S0-AIO-967

Beyond Existentialism and Zen

Beyond Existentialism and Zen

RELIGION IN A PLURALISTIC WORLD

GEORGE RUPP

New York
OXFORD UNIVERSITY PRESS
1979

Copyright © 1979 Oxford University Press, Inc.

Library of Congress Cataloging in Publication Data

Rupp, George.
Beyond existentialism and Zen.
Includes index.
1. Religion—Philosophy.   2. Apologetics—20th century.
3. Christianity and existentialism.
4. Zen Buddhism—Philosophy.   I. Title.
BL51.R68   200'.1   78-15681   ISBN 0-19-502463-1

Printed in the United States of America

Foreword

"Christian theology is in disarray." The first sentence of George Rupp's book immediately makes the reader wonder. Are we in for yet another hand-wringing indictment of the trespasses of modernity and the complicity of theology—before and after the fact—in assorted crimes and confusions? No: this is a very different kind of book indeed. Instead of scolding or hectoring, Rupp goes to work and explains with impressive cogency *why* theology is in disarray and *what* can be done to reestablish an element of coherence in what seems to have become a babble of monologues, soliloquies, and dialogues of the deaf. He has gone beyond both diagnosis and prescription and has traced out a perfectly plausible road map for the way ahead. The disarray need not be terminal.

Lest any prospective reader should mistakenly suppose that the argument here is merely for specialists, let it be said right at the outset that it surely is not. By "Zen and Existentialism" Rupp does not mean to restrict himself merely to the often elusive thought, for example, of D. T. Suzuki and Jean-Paul Sartre and their followers. The terms are used, rather, to designate two types of solutions to the central problem that modern religious thought faces. The problem itself is a two-headed one. On the one side all traditional sources of authority —Bible, Pope, tradition, religious experience—have been thrown into question, making it singularly difficult to resolve disputes or even to advance an argument. On the other side, more and more people now find themselves aware that we all live in a radically pluralistic world where once relatively isolated religious traditions now jostle each other on the same turf. This twofold challenge has come to Christianity, furthermore, just when humankind is faced by a whole series of new ethical questions—neutron bombs, test-tube babies, pollution and depletion, and possible impending famine—all of which call for a clear and unequivocal response from those charged with the responsibility of applying the religious and moral tradition from which our culture has emerged. Thus, just when our need for moral clarity is greater than ever before, we find that the trumpet is giving an uncertain sound. And uncertain trumpet calls do nothing but create further confusion and consternation in the ranks. George Rupp does not sound the trumpet, but (to extend the musical metaphor) although he has not composed a complete musical score, he has provided the key signature and the instrumentation so that the notes that must now be composed or played can have some harmonic, or at least contrapuntal, relationship to each other. In doing so he has performed a desperately needed service.

Rupp also describes two mistaken answers to the present crisis. As a student of contemporary religious and theological movements, I am all too aware of both of them, and of the destruction and befuddlement that have emerged in their wake. Neither dogmatism nor laissez-faire will do, he says, and he is right. To deal with rampant pluralism and the erosion of authority by retreating into a doctrinal redoubt like fundamentalists or by collapsing into mere relativism like some of the new pan-religious sects only makes the situation worse. Dogmatism reaches its comico-tragic denouement when biblicists and papists, traditionalists and experientialists, notice that no matter how hard they push their favored sources, and no matter how loudly they speak, no reasonable argument can even begin. There is only sound and fury. The relativist also notices sooner or later that despite the quaint modern prejudice that assigns equal worth to all opinions no matter how bizarre or reprehensible, one must eventually *live* by one truth or another. At this point relativism reaches its limit, or one of its limits. In addition, both relativism and dogmatism increasingly reveal themselves to be intellectual cop-outs, closely related refusals to deal patiently and thoughtfully with the most important and vexing questions of the age.

We do need some kind of authority, and it must be something a little more comprehensive than the experience of one individual. And we must not allow our healthy respect for pluralism to degenerate into what the older Catholic theology used to call "indifferentism." All religious roads do not lead to the same place. Like all roads anywhere, they lead to different places, and we had better know something about where they lead before we begin speeding along them. As Rupp points out so well, although it might once have seemed plausible to allow that Hinduism was just fine for India and Christianity for the west (a kind of "spheres of influence" solution), that way out simply does not work in an increasingly unified world culture. In the past one hundred and fifty years Christian communities have appeared in virtually every nation in the world, and Khrishna and the Buddha have their serious devotees in Portland and Boston as well as in Poona and Bangkok.

Rupp's contribution to a creative solution to the twin loss-of-authority/radical pluralism challenge is both simple and sophisticated. He asks us to remember that pluralism exists not only *among* but also *within* the various religious traditions. The conversation must go on not just between Christians and Buddhists, for example, but also among Christians and among Buddhists. This sounds so obvious at first that it seems to lead nowhere. But when the author goes on to clarify the philosophical premises that facilitate conversation among representatives of the various Christian bodies, two things become clearer. One is that some of these same principles can also be applied to dialogues with Moslems, Hindus, and other faiths. The other is that we may well discover there are schools of thought within this or that non-Christian religious tradition that seem in important ways closer to our own intepretation of Christianity than are certain opinions within Christianity itself. This could alter the contour of the conversation altogether. In some ways it suggests what occurs when card players change the game they are playing although they continue to use the same deck. Now suits or sequences become more important rather than high numbers or face cards. New possibilities emerge. Old deadlocks disappear. The same players and the same deck are still there. But it is an entirely new situation.

I learned a little about this "new deal" in inter-religious dialogue just before I read Rupp's book in the summer of 1978. I had made my first visit to Japan earlier that summer, in part to attend an international conference of religious scholars on the banning of nuclear weapons, and in part to hold conversations with Buddhist teachers and professors. One night I enjoyed a long and fruitful conversation with Professor Masao Abe, one of Japan's most prominent Buddhist thinkers, along with some of his colleagues and students, not all of whom were fully sympathetic to his Zen interpretation of Buddhism. Over a delicious dinner of tempura, seaweed dainties, and sake, I took delight in listening to the thrust and parry among the different Buddhist schools represented, noting especially that the Shin Buddhists (who represent one of the "Pure Land" schools to which Rupp devotes some attention in the latter part of Chapter III) felt that their insistence on the centrality of what they called "the other" was in some ways closer to Jewish and Christian thought than it was to certain interpretations in Zen. One Shin Buddhist scholar even went so far as to suggest, somewhat facetiously, that Zen was a kind of "religious porno," since, like sexual porno, it tended to focus on a single aspect of human experience to the virtual exclusion of other essential dimensions. He may have been incorrect, but his remark dramatized for me the radical differences one finds *among* Buddhists.

I got back to my hotel late and switched on the TV in my room. It had been pre-set by the hotel staff to the English language channel. Onto the screen flashed an American evangelist pleading for support from his viewers to convert those millions and millions of people in Japan who had not yet been won to the Gospel, since they were all lost and headed for hell and time was of the essence. I suddenly felt much closer to my hosts of the evening, especially to the Shin school Buddhists, than I did to my fellow Christian on the tube.

My experience in Japan was not an unusual one. I have met Buddhists, Hindus, and, of course, Jews to whom I have not only felt closer spiritually but with whom I have also agreed intellectually more than I do with many Christians. People of these historic faith groupings have occasionally confessed to me that they have felt the same way either about me or about some other Christian. Dietrich Bonhoeffer confesses in his *Letters and Papers from Prison* that he had the same feeling with nonreligious people. The experience is not uncommon. But what does it really mean theologically? This is the issue Rupp takes up and moves to a higher and infinitely more useful plane.

As I write this, the recent craze for meditation, usually packaged in "Oriental" dress, seems to have run its course. The first hints of a rebirth of Christian social concern are appearing along the murky horizon, not least among young evangelical Christians. What Rupp writes about as the challenge of existentialism—the need to respond in freedom to the challenge set by historical events to human existence —is in the air again. But the question inevitably suggests itself: Must we constantly bounce back and forth between Suzuki and Sartre? To reduce the question to the distorted form in which it often appears at the popular level, must we lurch between humorless commitment and vacuous withdrawal? Are Arthur Koestler's yogi and commissar the only available models?

Rupp's answer is a decided "no" to all the above. Not only can we move beyond Zen and existentialism, even more importantly, Christianity, rightly understood, can provide the vehicle by which we can do it: "The ideal to which the combined truths of existentialism and Zen point is . . . the double capacity to be fully and effectively invested in what one takes to be morally required activity and yet also to be able to stand back and laugh at oneself." Christianity has both a prophetic and a mystical dimension. Paradoxically, it can summon us to risk and endeavor and also remind us that ultimately we need only consider the lilies of the field to discover how little action is needed. Both sides are true, and at some level we all realize it.

Rupp warns us in the first sentence of his Preface that the argument of this book is demanding in the degree of sustained attention it will require from the reader. He is right. What I will add, however, is that it richly repays the effort it requires. It could be the book that will set the stage and supply the terms for what must surely happen theologically in the 1980's.

Harvey Cox

Preface

This study is a single sustained and at times perhaps even austere argument. As such, it is demanding in the attention it requires of the reader. What makes the argumentation taxing is, however, less its inherent difficulty than its aim of combining specialized analysis and generality of reference. Instead of expanding on each point in detail, I try to show the bearing of the argument on a representative spectrum of concerns. This procedure is not without its liabilities. But in a period of fragmented analysis, even a synoptic attempt to attain an overview is, I hope, enough of an asset to compensate for the relative paucity of illustration and elaboration entailed in this approach.

The austerity of presentation is most pronounced in the first chapter. There I discuss the methodological issues presupposed in the chapters that follow. I am convinced that such issues need to be addressed explicitly and self-consciously at some point in an analysis of religious commitment in the context of pluralism. But readers who prefer to begin with substantive rather than methodological concerns may want to proceed directly to the concluding sub-section of the first chapter entitled "Overview of the Argument." In that way they will move more immediately into the less specialized issues that the other chapters explore.

This book evolved in and through a number of other projects over a period of eight years. As a result, I have benefited from a great many discussions and suggestions in very diverse contexts. Informing the argument throughout the book have been conversations over the years with close friends: Donna and Bud Ogle; my wife, Nancy; Barbara Clark; Frank White. Also influential has been on-going feedback from student and faculty colleagues both at Johnston College in the University of Redlands, Redlands, California, and at Harvard Divinity School. Especially helpful have been criticism and suggestions from Bill and Dolores McDonald, Christopher Duraisingh, Harold Oshima, Sharon Parks, Harvey Cox, Arthur Dyck, Gordon Kaufman and Arthur McGill.

Of all those who have influenced the argument in this book, one person stands out: Wayne Proudfoot. He has provided detailed comments and suggests as the manuscript has evolved. But even more importantly, he and I have discussed the range of issues addressed in this book over a period of ten years, during which our thinking and writing developed along very similar lines. As I indicate in the notes, there are considerable parallels between the types outlined in the second and third chapters of this book and the positions developed in his *God and the Self: Three Types of Philosophy of Religion*. In my description of the three types, his influence is no doubt most evident. But even apart from such specific parallels, his broadly informed and critical intelligence have been a continuing source of stimulation.

For financial support at various stages of this project, I want to express my appreciation to the University of Redlands and the Ford Foundation for a faculty research award in the summer of 1972 and to Harvard University and the Association of Theological Schools for a sabbatical leave and a research grant in the spring and summer of 1976.

I want to thank all of the very helpful colleagues who have typed drafts and portions of this manuscript: Ruth Moran and Angela Sanabia in Redlands, California; Christine Langlais and Linda Kettner in Cambridge, Massachusetts; and Joanna Berentson in Green Bay, Wisconsin.

As I indicate in the notes when specific parallels are involved, this book is directly continuous with the more complex line of argument I advance in *Christologies and Cultures: Toward a Typology of Religious Worldviews*. In the few instances in which the same formulations appear in the first chapter of this book and the concluding chapter of *Christologies and Cultures,* those passages initially appeared in articles published some years ago. Accordingly, I want once again to express my gratitude to the following institutions for permission to include portions of articles which originally appeared under their auspices: to Temple University for several pages of my "Reader Response," *Journal of Ecumenical Studies,* 7 (1970), pp. 547-51; to the University Press of Hawaii for selected passages from my article, "The Relationship between Nirvāṇa and Saṃsāra: An Essay on the Evolution of Buddhist Ethics," *Philosophy East and West,* 21 (1971), pp. 55-67; and to the President and Fellows of Harvard College for excerpts from my essay, "Religious Pluralism in the Context of an Emerging World Culture," *The Harvard Theological Review,* 66 (1973), pp. 207-18.

All quotations from the Bible are from the Revised Standard Version, copyrighted 1946 and 1952 by the Division of Christian Education of the National Council of the Churches of Christ in the U.S.A.

Green Bay, Wisconsin
October 1978

G.R.

Contents

BEYOND EXISTENTIALISM AND ZEN

For Kathy and Stephanie

I

Theology in a Pluralistic World Culture

Christian theology is in disarray. Fads chase each other with unseemly haste. Drama flares as the death of God is announced (yet again) and even celebrated. Almost appropriately there follows a theology of hope. But then a theology of play? As the carrousel continues, one wishes it were a drunken revel, a carousal, rather than . . . a merry-go-round. Then at least there would be the prospect of the morning after, of sorting out the enduring from the ephemeral. As it is, the death of God, the rebirth of storytelling, theologies of hope, liberation, ecology, and play all seem to prance around with little direct relation to each other and no obviously significant differences in size or shape or composition or range of movement.

This conceit of the carrousel is, after all, just that—a conceit. But even if the image exaggerates, it is disquieting in the questions it focuses for contemporary theology: If the only differences among the horses are color and perhaps cleverly crafted appearances of disposition, why prefer one over the others? Besides, are not all the horses going the same way and to the same place—namely, nowhere? Every theologian is, of course, convinced that there are significant differences not only in style but also in substance among even contemporary interpretations of Christian faith. There may indeed be the possibility of some considerable consensus as to solid and valuable contributions. Yet there is no prospect for agreement on the norms and methods or even the content of the discipline. And radical disagreement on such underlying issues is what fosters the apprehension that theology is in fact only going around in circles.

3

There is, no doubt, ample confusion, even if attention is confined to Christian theology in the context of the West. But this restriction is itself becoming more and more problematical. Consequently, I want to explore the at least initially increased complexities that confront both religious commitment and theology or religious philosophy in an emerging world culture. Within this more inclusive context, my own particular interests do center on the Christian tradition. And much of the following analysis focuses on Christian and western developments. I am, however, persuaded that the situation of Christianity is in significant respects representative of problems that are increasingly common to the world's various religious and quasi-religious traditions. Accordingly, I attempt to generalize my remarks when it seems appropriate so that their applicability to multiple communities is evident.

Sources of the Contemporary Crisis in Christian Theology

Among the varied sources of the current crisis in Christian theology, two interrelated developments are, I submit, fundamental. The first is the relativization of every authority to which theology can appeal. And the second is the pervasive awareness of pluralism that characterizes contemporary culture. The two developments share a common and complexly connected history which bears directly on theology as the disciplined reflection of faith. This double development is, however, also at least indirectly relevant to even the least reflective stance of faith. The connection is through both theology and culture. Theology presupposes and is dependent on the believing community; but it also in turn influences the liturgical and ethical forms through which faith is shaped and expressed. As is the case with the influence of theology, the impact of a cultural ethos may be all the more powerful when there is little or no awareness of it. Accordingly, the relativization of authority and increased self-consciousness about pluralism are not only abstract and theoretical issues. Rather they are developments that in the end also inform the concrete and practical concerns of contemporary communities of faith.

In exploring the interrelated issues of relativism and pluralism, it is useful to keep in mind a simple and obvious but also profoundly significant difference between the current situation and that of first-century believers. This difference is susceptible of concise if unpalatable formulation: while first-century believers saw themselves as initiators, as the vanguard of a community of faith on the verge of eschatological confirmation, Christianity today at least appears to be what was once a great tradition well on its way to its demise. The contrast is, then, one of initiation and high expectations as opposed to a general sense of decline and perhaps termination.

Awareness of this difference in orientation is helpful in attempting to understand the attitudes of first-century Christians toward pluralism. The first century, no less than the twentieth, was a time of pervasive pluralism. The communities that came to be called Christian found themselves among innumerable cults centered on one or another deity or savior figure. To focus on the closest parallels, Christianity was one mystery religion among others that celebrated its dying and rising god.[1] Yet the community of converts—of those whose lives had been radically re-oriented, turned around, transformed—lived in the assurance that their faith would be vindicated. And insofar as the church was central to their lives, this faith was constantly reinforced by others who were equally convinced of its truth in spite of the fact that its power was not yet evident to those outside the community. There was, in short, what sociologists would term an effective plausibility structure to support their commitment.

In the period since the first century, the church has continued to provide a plausibility structure for believers. But with the development of its institutional standing in the culture, it has had changing resources on which to draw to support its credibility. Perhaps the most dramatic evolution is the shift from the assurance of expectation to the confidence of success. As the church came to prevail among the religious and cultural alternatives in the West, the truth of its beliefs seemed confirmed in the arena of history. Hence the church's own traditions and its power as an institution themselves became sources of authority.

With the waning of the power of the church as a discrete institution, a variety of apologetic strategies received increasing emphasis as supplementary or even alternative arguments for faith. Examples include appeals to the wisdom manifest in the order of creation, to miracle and prophecy, to a natural religion of reason, and to the inerrancy of the Bible. But the same developments that were corrosive of the institutional authority of the church—developments that have come to be termed secularism and individualism and, finally, relativism—in turn also rendered such further arguments problematical. The result has been that those forms of appeal which themselves address the issues of pluralism and secularism and relativism have in the last century increasingly dominated defenses of Christianity.

Two instances of such apologetic strategies are appeals to personal experience and to the achievements of western civilization. Appeal to personal experience as a strategy for addressing a pluralistic context is, of course, a perennial religious stance—and one reminiscent of the situation of the early church. Similarly, a positive appraisal of Christian contributions to western civilization suggests analogies to the role of the medieval church in shaping the culture of its time. Insofar as they are also indicative of the crisis in twentieth-century Christianity, the appeals to personal experience and to the achievements of the West may, therefore, serve to illustrate the changed situation in the present.

In contrast to the first-century believer's confidence of membership in a body of the threshold of triumphant vindication, Christians today must affirm their faith as one among multiple perspectives that have re-emerged after the disintegration of the church's pre-eminence. Even sectarian communities committed to continuing a shared identity that structures their lives as a whole cannot completely avoid contact with an encompassing (and often invading) culture that insistently poses the question of whether believers represent vestiges of the past rather than being harbingers of the future. Accordingly, appeal to religious experience no longer finds support in the assurance that those outside the community of faith have simply not yet heard and believed the good news. Instead, religious experience appears even to many believers as very much an individual, even an idiosyncratic, affair. This development, of course, threatens not only the church but also individual faith, since it must sustain itself without benefit of the plausibility structure that is available to persons when their lives are organized around or centered in an explicitly shared and constantly reinforced common identity.

Similarly, appeal to the dynamism of western civilization has less force the more peripheral the church is to that culture. One can (I think rightly) argue that Christian traditions have been crucial for the development of a host of western institutional patterns and disciplines including much of the impetus toward capitalist economic organization, political democracy, the formation of voluntary associations, and the emergence of the modern natural sciences. This argument still leaves the serious problem of Christian involvement in and responsibility for the atrocities attendant on this complex of developments. But even apart from the finally intractable moral issues involved, this line of argument in any case does not in itself provide a persuasive apologetic for the contemporary relevance of Christianity. Hegemony in the past does not, in short, alter the increasingly marginal status of the church in the present as one institution among many with no exclusive claim on even such bastions of its mission as education and social welfare.

Dogmatism and the Varieties of Relativism

The crisis confronting contemporary theology is, then, rooted in historical patterns which have developed over many centuries and which at least appear to be irreversible. In any case, the collapse of traditional authorities and the radical pluralism of today's culture show no signs of reversing themselves in the foreseeable future. Accordingly, the question for theology is what role it has to play in this situation of systematic pluralism and relativized authority.

Two apparently antithetical approaches to answering this question initially suggest themselves. The first is to advocate a position which can be claimed to be immune to the critique of relativism. And the second is to accept an unqualified relativism as unavoidable. As different as the positions of dogmatic pronouncement and unqualified relativism may appear, their recent formulations in fact proceed from a number of shared premises. This common ground is especially marked in their often only implicit presuppositions about the nature and the limits of knowledge. To state this contention in simplified form so as to focus the issue with reference to recent western thought: both positions assume a Kantian epistemological model.

For Kant human knowledge is programmatically limited to the phenomenal world or the world of appearances. This world includes all of existence in space and time, and within that frame of reference there is knowledge Kant wants to defend as objective in the sense that it is universal and necessary for all human subjects. But precisely because this knowledge presupposes the human perceptual and cognitive constitution, it cannot attain to the noumenal as opposed to the phenomenal realm or the thing in itself as opposed to appearances in space and time. About that, the human subject can claim no knowledge whatsoever.

The model is, then, one of inviolable limits, of insurmountable barriers, which confine human knowers to the world of appearances and separate them programmatically and completely from the real as such. Kant himself would no doubt be chagrined to see his reflections on the limits of theoretical reason employed in the service of either unqualified relativism or dogmatic theology. After all, his efforts were directed toward establishing the objectivity of empirical knowledge and protecting the claims of rational or moral religion. Yet both unqualified relativism and recent dogmatics do at least tacitly assume this epistemological model. The connection is perhaps more evident in the case of total relativism. In this instance, the divorce between the phenomenal and the noumenal implies that no claim to knowledge about reality as such can be preferred to any other. The same model may, however, also underlie those positions which purport to be immune from the corrosive effects of relativism. Certainly the most influential twentieth-century Christian illustration of this possibility is the line of argument which Karl Barth advances in his *The Epistle to the Romans*. Barth includes Christianity with all other religious traditions as historically relative expressions of human arrogance forever doomed to failure in their attempts to attain to the truth of God. Consequently Christian faith or the Gospel as the expression of the action of God must in Barth's view be systematically distinguished from all such historical traditions including Christianity: divine revelation alone provides access to that truth from which every human effort to know is infinitely distant.

To contend that the relativity of all perspectives precludes discrimination among positions because they are all absolutely incommensurable with the real and the true seems somehow arbitrary. Similarly, to distinguish the revelation of God proclaimed in the Christian Gospel from all religions seems contrived. And in both cases, the sense of artificiality is justified because the epistemology informing those positions is untenable.

The difficulty in the epistemological model is already specified in Hegel's definitive and, I think, incontrovertible critique of Kant's position. Hegel again and again argues that the dichotomy between phenomenal knowledge and noumenal reality is untenable in the strict sense that it cannot be formulated without contradiction. Insofar as human subjects conceive of and talk about the thing in itself or noumenal reality, they already relate it to other forms of awareness or consciousness including that of empirical objects. There is, in short, no absolute distinction between what is available to human knowing and reality as such. Instead, all claims to knowledge are more or less successful attempts to grasp or comprehend the real itself. It is, to be sure, useful and even necessary to distinguish between the object as it is in the consciousness of the knower and the thing in itself. But while the intention of this distinction is to call attention to the limitations of a given claim to knowledge, its effect is to drive the knower toward more adequate comprehension. The epistemological model is not, then, one of the knower on one side of an inpenetrable barrier and reality on the other. Instead there is an ongoing process of interaction between the knower and the real, a process which in principle acknowledges no limits even if in practice it can never attain that ideal of totally adequate comprehension which Hegel termed "absolute knowledge" or "the truth."[2]

This Hegelian critique of Kant provides resources for rejecting both dogmatism and unqualified relativism in favor of a third more adequate position. This third position acknowledges the truth of relativism. It recognizes the rootedness of every position in particular personal, social, and cultural conditions. Yet because the various partial and incomplete perspectives are attempts at grasping or comprehending the one reality there is, it is possible to make judgments as to their measure of validity. In short, this position qualifies the relativism which it affirms because it introduces a dimension of criticism toward all claims including its own. The task of articulating and defending criteria for this critical and comparative enterprise is, to be sure, extremely complex and itself subject to appraisal. But because the reality toward which claims of truth are directed is not by definition completely inaccessible, this task is not proscribed in principle.

Critical Relativism and Diversity Within Traditions

The position of critical relativism is not only epistemologically more sound than the alternatives of dogmatism and unqualified relativism; it is also able to account more accurately for the practice of Christian theologians and those in comparable positions of intellectual responsibility in other communities. This ability is especially evident if one focuses on diversity within traditions—diversity illustrated both in disagreements at a given time and in differences from period to period. For the very fact of change or development in both doctrine and practice counters the presumption that any religious position has attained immutable truth in favor of an approach which recognizes the historical particularity and relativity of both reflective interpretations and institutional patterns. And the persistence of controversy in the history of religious communities indicates that theologians and other religious thinkers have construed their task as the attempt to express truth rather than as the articulation of one among multiple possible and equally valid perspectives. In appropriating the traditions of their communities, theologians and their equivalents in nontheistic frames of reference have, in short, sought to interpret doctrine and practice so as to formulate the truth to which they are committed as cogently and powerfully as possible in varying historical contexts and in opposition to a changing array of alternative positions.

The fact that a critical relativism can do justice to the practice of even the most traditional Christian theology should not, however, obscure the equally significant fact that this position was not self-consciously and explicitly articulated at least among western religious thinkers until the modern period. Diversity in views is not without antecedents in every tradition. But the pervasive and self-conscious awareness of pluralism characteristic of contemporary culture and the attempt to analyze the relativism implied in that awareness have fewer precedents. The occasion for such analysis in recent western history has been the fragmentation of a once more unified culture—a situation which is very different not only from the encounter of Christian faith with first-century Hellenistic culture but also from the interaction of a self-confident church with the heritage of Platonic philosophy in the patristic period or with Aristotelianism and Islamic thought in the High Middle Ages.

Greater self-consciousness about pluralism has the effect of radicalizing its impact. Unreflective awareness that other people adhere to different traditions becomes instead a recognition of multiple perspectives as alternatives competing for the individual's allegiance. This personalizing of pluralism is especially pronounced once believers or devotees see that there is a plurality of positions even within the nominally unified tradition to which they are committed. For then they are confronted with the need to make judgments of relative adequacy whether or not they maintain their adherence to this tradition.

Increasing awareness of the need to make such judgments even if one remains loyal to a particular tradition is of course an index of how pervasive is the sense of pluralism on the contemporary religious scene. It is, however, also a significant extension of the dynamics of pluralism precisely because it allows an appraisal of alternatives apart from the trauma of completely renouncing prior commitments. Hence the question becomes more complex than simply whether or not, for example, to remain a Christian as opposed to identifying with Buddhism or Marxism or agnostic humanism. Instead, the issue in this case also involves the different varieties of Christianity.

That there is diversity to the point even of opposition within any single religious tradition need not be belabored. Two examples may, however, serve to epitomize how fundamental are the issues which divide adherents of the same tradition. The first is the question of whether salvation as the goal of the religious life is an individual or a communal and ultimately universal affair. The second is the question of whether historical existence is of intrinsic value or only of instrumental worth as a means to a finally superhistorical end. To speak only of the two traditions with which I am most familiar, each response to these two questions has its contemporary advocates among both Buddhists and Christians.

With reference to the first question, the tendency of modern Christian pietism and moralism is toward a soteriological individualism, while ecclesiastical orthodoxy insists more unambiguously on an at least potentially universal work of salvation effected through the life and death of Christ. Lutheran Rudolf Bultmann's theological existentialism is a radical and consistent example of the individualistic tendency; and the thought of a contemporary Roman Catholic like Karl Rahner illustrates commitment to universalism. The differences between Theravāda and Mahāyāna Buddhists provide a similar contrast. Theravādins typically view religious fulfillment as the attainment of individuals through their own effort and discipline. In contrast, at least one important tendency in the soteriology of the Mahāyāna insists that all of existence is ingredient in that ultimate reality which is the goal of the religious life. The writings of U. Thittila and D. T. Suzuki illustrate the Theravāda and the Mahāyāna positions, respectively.

An analogous plurality of perspectives is evident in Buddhist and Christian reflection on the second question. For Theravādins like K. N. Jayatilleke or Nyanaponika Thera historical existence is religiously significant only as the medium through which superhistorical truth or reality is attained. Insofar as the characteristic Mahāyāna position affirms that the ultimately real is precisely phenomenal existence rightly apprehended, there is already a general disagreement with the Theravāda perspective. But in the thinking of such Japanese Buddhists as Kenneth Inada and Susumu Yamaguchi, both of whom are conversant with western philosophical and religious traditions, there is in addition the contention that historical processes themselves are intrinsically significant because the ideal of fully realized existence is in fact undergoing actualization through those historical processes. Despite the potentially positive value ascribed to the historical order through the doctrine of creation, Christian faith reveals a similar double-mindedness. On the one hand, belief in a wholly other God, in the transhistorical efficacy of Christ's work as a transaction accomplished once for all, and in heavenly fulfillment for the faithful all counter the affirmation that historical existence is itself of intrinsic value. Among twentieth-century theologians many emphases in the thought of Karl Barth express this tendency. On the other hand, such movements as the American social gospel ascribe value to temporal life precisely because it is susceptible of progressive transformation into what is ultimately the full realization of the kingdom of God. Among the most consistent contemporary representatives of this general perspective is Wolfhart Pannenberg.[3]

This plurality of positions among more or less official or at least professional religious thinkers is not without its effects on their respective communities. Perhaps the most crucial result is that reflective believers or devotees are increasingly in the position of self-consciously having to fashion their own interpretations of the institutional forms, ritual actions, images, and ideas mediated through the tradition to which they are committed. Reflective believers are, in short, involved in the enterprise of theology or religious philosophy. They may learn from the work of professional theologians and their counterparts in other traditions but to an unprecedented degree they also participate in constructive religious or theological reflection themselves—with the further proliferation of perspectives that this participation implies.

Pluralism in an Emerging World Culture

To distinguish multiple perspectives within each tradition is of course to attend to only one set of the variables involved in exploring the issue of religious pluralism. To approach the issue through this set of variables is, however, salutary in at least two respects. First it calls attention to distinctions that are easily ignored, since the issue of religious pluralism is frequently formulated with reference simply to the traditions as such. And second, it provides a serviceable prism for focusing the issue because the dynamics of pluralism as they are present in the appraisal of alternatives within an ostensibly unified tradition are in fact remarkably analogous to the more complex interaction between different traditions.

In the past it has been possible to overlook or obscure this parallelism with the contention that the various religious traditions perform the same function for their respective cultures. In contrast to less grandiose versions of the same position, such unqualified relativism on the scale of whole religious systems or entire cultures has had the advantage of relative isolation among the perspectives which are purported to be equally valid. Consequently it has seemed plausible to view the various religious systems as adapted to the particular needs of different cultures. A critical presupposition of this interpretation has, however, been the existence of more or less discrete cultures. And precisely this presupposition is less and less valid.

Differentiable traditions of course continue to exist. But they interact in an increasingly shared history. Crucial to this development has been the impetus of those processes of modernization that arose initially in the West. Complementing continued Asian and African interest in western political institutions and patterns of economic organization are, however, considerable cultural and in particular religious influences in both directions. The result is continued and at times even intensified pluralism within all traditions even as an incipient world culture seems to be emerging.

Consideration of comparisons and contrasts between traditions in addition to the diversity within each tradition in the first instance seems only to multiply the variables with which an interpretation of religious pluralism must come to terms. That initial impression is, however, misleading if it suggests only a further proliferation of differences. For insofar as the issues which separate perspectives within one community have parallels in other traditions, they may indicate similarities which are not at first evident. If one abstracts from specific images, conceptions, institutions, and rituals, there may, in short, be greater commonality in systematic commitments or tendencies between some adherents of different traditions than among the full variety of perspectives within a single tradition. To refer again to the contemporary Buddhist and Christian thinkers already used illustratively, there may be more systematic common ground between the universalism of both Karl Rahner and D. T. Suzuki than between Suzuki and a Theravādin like U. Thittila or between Rahner and a radical individualist like Bultmann. Conversely, there may be a greater systematic contrast between the transhistorical tendencies of Karl Barth's thought and the emphatically historical approach of Wolfhart Pannenberg than there is between Pannenberg and an at least incipiently historically oriented Mahāyānist like Susumu Yamaguchi or between Barth and a Theravādin who insists that historical existence must be conquered and transcended, as does Nyanaponika Thera.

Illustrations could, of course, be multiplied indefinitely, especially if one compared and contrasted positions from different historical periods instead of focusing only on contemporary thinkers. But even a very few examples suggest how the existence of a multiplicity of perspectives within ostensibly unified traditions in combination with the increasing interaction entailed in an emerging world culture serve to establish the context for any systematic and at least potentially comprehensive interpretation of religious pluralism. Within this context what is needed is, then, an analysis of alternatives in each tradition so that the process of interaction among the various communities may measure the very disparate degrees of similarity and differences depending on which of the perspectives in the two traditions are compared and contrasted.

To underscore the implications of this approach to religious pluralism, it may be useful to note the points of agreement and disagreement with the frequently advanced if somewhat facile assertion that the various religious perspectives and correlative practices are simply different paths or ways to the same ultimate destination. This position is inadequate because it does not do justice to the situation of pluralism even within a single tradition. To refer once more to the issues already used as examples, it is not a matter of indifference whether the end to which all traditions are allegedly means is conceived as an individually achieved goal or as a universal reality, as an eternal destination transcending time or as the *telos* of historical development itself. Hence a more accurate aphorism would be: each of the various religious traditions includes different approaches leading to different goals. Yet this suggestion of an unqualified pluralism is also an oversimplification, inasmuch as it abstracts from the possibility of parallels between systematically analogous perspectives in different traditions. There is in this sense a need to assent to the insight that the various traditions are different means to the same end, for there may be perspectives in two different traditions which are systematically parallel even when the dominant tendencies of each tradition are radically opposed. As a result, it is entirely possible that greater antagonism and opposition in principle exist between some alternative positions within a tradition than between selected perspectives of completely different communities. Perhaps the most dramatic contemporary illustration of this possibility centers on the question of whether or not religious leaders and institutions should be involved directly in social, economic, and political activities. But a similar parallelism in conflicts within traditions is also discernible on such more strictly religious and philosophical issues as the question of whether salvation is an individual or a finally universal affair.

The approach to the question of religious pluralism which I am proposing is not, then, one which attempts to unify all possible perspectives. Nor does it simply pronounce them all equally valid. Instead, it analyzes similarities and differences and then makes choices which in turn entail criticism of the rejected alternatives. The choices are not, however, judgments which simply discriminate between traditions. For a recognition of multiple perspectives within the various communities offers the prospect of discerning common systematic commitments even in apparently very different traditions. In this connection the process of interaction between communities is of special importance because it may serve to intensify the self-consciousness of what might be minor or even submerged tendencies if the tradition in question remained isolated. The result may be a provisional increase in diversity—but one which includes the prospect of a commonality transcending traditional divisions.

Norms for Appraising Alternatives

Talk about criticism and choice presupposes the availability of norms for adjudicating among alternatives both within the same tradition and in different traditions. The process of appraisal is not identical in the two cases. But they can appropriately be discussed together because the central pattern of contemporary interaction among perspectives within a tradition is also applicable to the process of mutual evaluation between positions from different traditions.

Appraisal of alternative perspectives claiming to represent the same tradition requires a double judgment as to relative adequacy. First, there must be a determination as to whether or not the position advanced is persuasive in its claim to speak for the tradition in question. Positive appraisal on this score is a matter of historical necessity: unless the position under scrutiny is acceptable to adherents of the tradition it purports to represent, it has no authority in the empirical sense that it exercises no power over the believers or devotees of its community. While positive judgment on this question of fidelity to tradition is necessary, it is not, however, the sufficient condition of adequacy, because there are multiple discrete and in some cases systematically opposed positions that can satisfy this requirement. Accordingly, a further judgment is needed as to the truth of the position both in interpreting and in turn in shaping contemporary experience.

The works of Christian theologians and of those in comparable positions of intellectual responsibility and religious authority in other traditions illustrate both kinds of appeal. References to the tradition and either implicit or explicit claims to represent that tradition on the one hand and arguments about capacity to illuminate salient features of contemporary life on the other of course appear in greatly differing ratios. In the Christian tradition, for example, dogmatic and philosophical theology suggest poles between which there is a spectrum of approaches. And even in those traditions for which the designation "dogmatic" is invariably pejorative, there nonetheless is also a combining, in differing ratios, of appeals to tradition and to contemporary experience.

That the two appeals are combined in virtually all theology or religious philosophy is significant in that it calls attention to the mutually reinforcing character of the two lines of argument. Insofar as a tradition continues to be vital, it unavoidably shapes the experience of its adherents so that their very awareness is at least in part structured through the institutional forms, ritual actions, images, and ideas comprising the religious system in question. As a result, appeals to tradition and to contemporary experience in fact occur in complex interconnections, even though the two patterns are distinguishable for analytic purposes.

The last court for adjudicating both forms of appeal is the arena not of abstract argument but of concrete historical developments. In the end, whether a position is or is not accepted as a vital expression of the tradition it claims to represent is subject to empirical confirmation. Similarly, the ability of a particular perspective or even the symbolism of an entire tradition to interpret contemporary experience persuasively and shape it effectively is also a matter of historical demonstration. Yet despite the fact that final appraisal is subject to the judgment of history, religionists show little inclination simply to wait and see which perspectives ultimately prevail. Instead tome upon tome and not a few tombs through the centuries testify to an intense interest in anticipating the end.

There are reprehensible instances of forced conversion and persecution of heretics in the history of religious disputations. But this history also evidences a commitment to serious appraisal of alternatives —a commitment which reflective believers and devotees must continue precisely because religious traditions can and do exercise profound influences on human culture. To continue this commitment is not, however, simply to repeat past practice. Instead there is a definite tendency in recent religious thought to reverse the relative priority typically assigned in the past to appeals to tradition and to contemporary experience. Especially in cases of forced conversion or persecution of heresy, there has been a very strong emphasis on fidelity to tradition. In contrast, recent theology and religious philosophy focus much more centrally on the power of the positions they advocate to interpret contemporary experience coherently and shape or influence it effectively.

There are multiple reasons for this reversal of priorities. A crucial consideration is the increasing awareness of participants in religious communities that their traditions change and develop. Insofar as believers or devotees acknowledge the developmental character of every religious system including their own, they in effect more or less self-consciously subordinate appeals to tradition to the norm of adequacy to contemporary experience. The difference from earlier generations of the faithful is, however, more one of self-consciousness than of actual practice, for tradition as such has never been available apart from its appropriation and interpretation in the present consciousness of believers or devotees. Yet changed self-consciousness does in turn affect behavior. If it is acknowledged that there is no fixed standard against which to measure deviance, heresy-hunting becomes less appealing. Similarly, as the role of birth and historical circumstance in influencing religious affiliation is more explicitly recognized, the central issue for reflective believers or devotees is not so much which tradition they should choose as it is to which of the alternatives within a given tradition they should commit themselves.

Insofar as the appraisal of alternatives within a tradition appeals centrally to the norm of adequacy to contemporary experience, this process of evaluation and that involved in adjudicating between perspectives in different traditions become increasingly similar. For of the two norms involved in sorting out disputes within a tradition, only the second one is directly relevant to comparisons and contrasts between perspectives in different traditions. Adherents of the various perspectives may of course appeal to the authority of their respective traditions. But the relative truth of precisely those traditions is what is under consideration. Accordingly, the decisive appeal can be only to the power of each perspective in interpreting and shaping the increasingly common experience which the various traditions share. In short, the parallelism in the dynamics of pluralism within and between traditions is evident in the respective processes of appraisal as well.

Interaction Between Traditions

So far the need to determine relative adequacy to contemporary experience has been expressed only in very general terms. What is required now is some specification of the criteria informing this judgment about the relative truth of differing positions. One approach to isolating criteria that in fact allow comparisons and contrasts between very diverse perspectives is to observe the dynamics of interaction between adherents of different religious traditions. Such interaction is not, of course, confined to the situation of direct conversation between believers or devotees of the various traditions. Instead, it occurs whenever persons who self-consciously subscribe to definite values or beliefs or patterns of action appraise a perspective other than their own. The printed word and, in pluralistic cultures, direct observation are, therefore, widespread media for such interaction. But the paradigm of personal conversation between adherents of different traditions may nonetheless serve to indicate the multiple directions from which the question of truth is in practice raised.

As the following description of such conversation or dialogue attempts to indicate, I am persuaded that the forms of argument typically expressed in this process of mutual appraisal can usefully be correlated with the formal criteria of truth in the western philosophical tradition. No doubt the process of dialogue may be described with reference to other evaluative rubrics as well. But the correspondence, coherence, and pragmatic criteria of truth may serve to illustrate how such formal categories in fact shape the appraisal of adequacy to contemporary experience.

The dynamics of interaction in dialogue among adherents of different religious perspectives presuppose that even though understanding and consequent appreciation are not absent, evaluation is not normally positive without qualification. Perhaps the most frequent form of initial dissatisfaction is expressed as an appeal to ostensibly shared premises. The contention that certain beliefs—in a transcendent personal deity or in transmigration, for example—are simply incredible if one accepts generally established scientific hypotheses illustrates this appeal. So, too, does questioning the ethical implications of a belief or a complex of beliefs and practices because they seem to violate universally accepted values or norms. Any such appeal to allegedly shared premises may, however, be premature if it is made with reference to a particular commitment abstracted from the religious system as a whole. This possibility is most readily apparent in the second line of criticism. A Buddhist may, for example, argue that the substantial and immortal soul in which at least some Christians believe unavoidably entails a preoccupation with the self and its eternal destiny—a self-preoccupation which is held to be destructive of genuine spirituality. Or a Muslim may charge that the Hindu view of phenomenal existence as ultimately illusory undermines any serious concern with concrete social and ethical problems. The initial criticism is, in short, on a pragmatic level: a belief or a practice is appraised negatively because it at least seems to conflict with values which the critic espouses. But in examining the ramifications of any specific criticism, the dialogue partners see that there are numerous interconnections between the particular point at issue and other commitments of the religious system. Hence the initial use of what is in effect a pragmatic criterion of truth results in a systematic evaluation of each dialogue partner's position as a unified religious perspective.

Evaluation at this level is, then, a combining of the initial pragmatic criterion with judgments about the coherence of the system as a whole. In this process of appraisal one way in which further interconnections among the beliefs and practices constituting the religious system become evident is in response to questions about experiences which seem to contradict the religious commitments under scrutiny. In that sense a correspondence theory of truth is operative: the critic indicates data of experience which seem to conflict with the religious tenet in question. But the response to such queries typically is an argument to the effect that further resources in the religious tradition can account for the apparent difficulty. As a result, the criterion of correspondence functions in the first instance only to provide the impetus for elaborating the full complexity of the religious system. Once that system is articulated in some detail, the criterion of correspondence may again be employed. But at this level, the correspondence theory no longer conforms to the paradigm of perception of an empirical object—verification of whether the pole with one end in the water and the other above the surface is in fact bent, for example. Instead, the question of correspondence has reference to wholes of experience.

At this point, then, the truth question becomes an appraisal of the adequacy to contemporary experience in the sense in which I have been using that phrase. The issue is the degree to which the religious system offers a coherent interpretation of the whole of human experience and thereby effectively shapes the thoughts, affections, and actions of its adherents in what is deemed a constructive direction. Adjudication of this issue unavoidably involves values which themselves are not exempt from criticism, since the question of what direction is constructive patently entails an appeal which itself requires legitimation. But this requirement only underscores the fact that the process of evaluation is mutual; it does not invalidate the process itself.

Assessment of religious systems ranging from the most primitive to the most complex of contemporary world traditions may be construed as conforming to this pattern. To take a very general example from traditional religious symbolism, the fact that agricultural societies preoccupied with the question of fertility frequently conceive of ultimate principles as feminine in character while patriarchal, pastoral cultures affirm masculine deities renders highly dubious a claim that either view offers a literal formulation of absolute truth. Nonetheless, both religious systems serve to interpret the world which their adherents experience. In this sense they have reference to the facts of particular forms of social and personal life. Hence they may legitimately claim some measure of validity, even if it is limited in scope. This recognition or consciousness of limitation is, however, precisely what differentiates the present religious situation from even the relatively recent past. Because twentieth-century peoples are increasingly aware of each other's experience, any such provincial validity is no longer viable. Instead the full diversity of human living is integral to that increasingly common or shared experience which every religious system interprets and in turn shapes.

The effect of the process of dialogue is, then, to call into question those commitments of a tradition which are less than universal in at least potential reference. In focusing awareness of the cultural relativity of every position, interaction with another tradition serves as an impetus to reinterpret or even to modify existing commitments in the direction of greater comprehensiveness. Hence dialogue between religious traditions is not only an academic exercise in mutual understanding. It is also a process through which constructive change can occur in the participants' interpretation of their own positions as they attempt to respond to the critical appraisal which their partners offer.

To construe the purpose of dialogue as the achievement of more adequate religious systems no doubt places a positive valuation on this possibility of modifications in each participant's self-understanding. This emphasis should not, however, be confused with a policy of syncretism. Dialogue does, to be sure, presuppose that both partners in principle recognize that they can benefit from conversation with each other. One can also assume that alterations in the direction of greater comprehensiveness will increase the measure of common ground which different traditions share. But in contrast to the product resulting from a process of syncretism, each tradition will continue to

exemplify an integrity of its own because any modifications are rein-
terpretations or adaptations of its own images, conceptions, and
practices. The result is not an incongruous combination of incompatible elements but a new synthesis which is continuous with a living
and therefore developing tradition.

Mahatma Gandhi and Martin Luther King provide vivid twentieth-century illustrations of this synthetic power—and also of the
cumulative effect of interaction between religious traditions. Neither
attempted to integrate all the commitments of a number of different
systems. Instead, each man appropriated insights or emphases complementary to his own particular convictions from one or more other
traditions; in the process each fashioned a richer though nonetheless
still unified religious worldview which stands in direct (even if frequently critical) relation to the tradition in which it is nurtured.
Dialogue will not, of course, create a Gandhi or a King. But their
lives and thought nonetheless exemplify in striking form the potential
for increasing the depth and power of one religious tradition through
creative interaction with another. To judge the realization of this potential as generally desirable assumes that no tradition has an interest
in celebrating or perpetuating inadequacies in any other religious system. Those who seek deficiencies in other traditions in order to con-
firm their belief in the superiority of their own may dispute this assumption. But one can hope that this tendency will be one of the first
casualties of genuine dialogue between adherents of different religious traditions.

Relativism, Pluralism, and Theological Method

Dialogue as a process of mutual appraisal directed toward the
achievement of more adequate religious systems is, then, an illustration of the approach to pluralism, both within and between traditions,
which I have referred to as critical relativism. The context for such
dialogue—namely, interaction within an increasingly common or
shared history—is also the context for contemporary Christian theology. Indeed, the process of dialogue and the enterprise of constructive
theology are in many respects systematically analogous. It remains,
however, to indicate with specific reference to Christian theology the
method or procedure which this parallelism suggests.

As is illustrated in its own past practice, and as is in any case unavoidable if the strictures of relativism are recognized, Christian theology begins with the particular experience of those who participate in Christian traditions. At the same time, this reflection rooted in particular traditions insists that the proper concern of theology is the whole of reality. To be sure, theology that expresses a critical and self-critical relativism can and indeed must insist with the prophets and the mystics that no product of human thought or action is finally adequate to the truth or reality of God. Yet this affirmation of iconoclasm and ultimate mystery does not posit a reality utterly separate from that life in space and time in which human selves are involved. Instead the theologian seeks to interpret precisely this experienced reality in its most encompassing context.

The images, the ideas, and the ritual and institutional patterns that constitute the traditions of the church themselves decisively shape the experience that the theologian seeks to interpret. The experience of the theologian is not, however, confined to those traditions, especially in the context of contemporary pluralism. One indication of this fact is the extent to which the setting for Christian theology increasingly is the secular university as well as or even instead of the church. This development represents a very complex evolution under the pressure of many sometimes conflicting forces. It is, moreover, a development entailing serious threats to the entire enterprise of Christian self-reflection—threats which may be epitomized in a tendency to retreat from all constructive theological work as incommensurate with the canons of the university. But whatever its ambiguities, the double institutional context of university and church testifies to the imperative that theology not become a function simply of the community of the faithful. Instead of any such withdrawal to an institutional context that is becoming more and more peripheral to contemporary life, Christian theology must continue its traditional commitment both to interpret and to address the whole of culture.

One task of theology is, then, to reflect on the dynamics of contemporary life which have particular relevance to religious concerns. In engaging in this task, theology can appropriate the learning of a variety of other disciplines. Indeed, because the concern of theology is with the whole of reality, no area of knowledge is irrelevant to it. The fact that theology and philosophy share this holistic intention helps to explain their interdependence through the centuries. But theology also has more particular interests. A crucial case in point is its preoccupation with the constitution and the transformation of individuals and their communities. In the differentiation of western academic disciplines, this area of investigation has gradually become institutionalized apart from both theology and philosophy. But the knowledge at which the social sciences aim is nonetheless directly and intimately related to theology. Accordingly, theology can now abandon those domains to secular disciplines only at the price of isolating itself from relevant empirical data in its pronouncements about human nature and destiny. The social sciences are, in short, an increasingly important resource for the theological task of reflecting on the personal, social, and cultural context within which the life of the Christian community takes place.

A second task for theologians derives from the fact that included in their experience is the awareness of others who also seek to interpret and respond to all of reality, but from different perspectives. This further task is that of abstracting from the concrete detail of experience in order to clarify one's own position and to focus systematic issues through comparison with alternative approaches. This process of critical comparison of one's own perspective with the various tendencies in one's own and other traditions is a form of interaction with those other perspectives. And as in the process of dialogue, the result (even if not always the intention) of this interaction is to increase both the self-consciousness of those involved and the range of resources available to them.

Helpful in outlining alternatives on definite systematic issues is the elaboration of types or generalized positions, each having numerous instances and variations. If the benefits of this approach are to be realized, however, it is crucial to be aware of its limitations as well. Those limitations derive from the fact that types are abstractions. To abstract or generalize from concrete and particular data may be illuminating—in this case, as a process for clarifying and focusing systematic issues. But abstractions also distort data insofar as their status as abstractions is obscured or overlooked. For instance, a generalized type may be employed to indicate systematic common ground between a particular Buddhist and a particular Christian perspective. This procedure does not, however, entail the contention that there are no differences between the two positions or that the type can replace both positions. Instead, as a deliberate simplification of experience so that systematic alternatives on central issues may be identified, every typology patently presupposes the complex dynamics of the concrete and varied traditions from which it is abstracted.

A third theological task is evident in this dependence of all general types on particular traditions. This task is what many Christians would consider the proper, or even the only, assignment of theology. It is the expression of the truth of faith for today. This task entails the appropriation of particular symbolic resources in the tradition so as to interpret and in turn to shape the concrete dynamics of contemporary life. This task is no doubt central to the theological enterprise. If it is to be an active appropriation of the tradition rather than a repetition of past forms, it must, however, be approached as self-conscious and creative participation in a complex tradition that continues to develop. And for theology so conceived, this third constructive enterprise cannot be separated from the descriptive and comparative interests of the other two tasks.

Overview of the Argument

The remainder of this book is an attempt to do theology of the sort I have sketched. The next two chapters undertake the two preliminary tasks I have indicated. In specifying the more inclusive context which theological reflection presupposes, I refer in some detail to an essay by sociologist Robert Bellah. I then outline a typology of what I see as the systematic alternatives for responding to the situation that I think Bellah accurately describes. Included in this discussion are my reasons for considering one of the typological positions more adequate than the others. Finally, I seek to show how Christian traditions may be interpreted so as to express the typological alternative I advocate.

The ordering of the argument in this book lends itself to a criticism which I should like to anticipate. The criticism is that the Christian theological perspective I advance in the final chapter is simply a function of or derivative from one of the typological positions I outline. The perspective expressed in that chapter does illustrate the third alternative in the typology discussed in the preceding two chapters. It is not, however, a function of or derivative from the third type because the typology itself presupposes precisely such particular perspectives in generalizing systematic alternatives. That my discussion of the third type focuses on the philosophy of Hegel no doubt complicates the situation. But since Hegel himself self-consciously attempts to grasp the truth of Christianity in his philosophy, the priority of historical religious traditions in relation to conceptual systematizations in any case remains.

To validate its claim to the title of Christian theology, the position I affirm in the final chapter must be able to demonstrate its continuity with central commitments of this religious community. As I have indicated in discussing the norms for appraising alternative perspectives, this demonstration of fidelity to tradition is, however, only the necessary, not the sufficient, condition of theological validity. The reason for the limitation on the appeal to tradition is, as I have argued, a simple and direct one: there are multiple discrete and in some cases systematically opposed positions which can satisfy this condition. As a result, the norm of adequacy to the whole of experience must complement that of effectiveness in representing the tradition. And precisely this issue is the one I address in commending the third of the typological alternatives in Chapter III. Accordingly, my advocacy of the position I articulate in the final chapter requires not only the demonstration in that chapter of its capacity to represent the Christian tradition but also the preceding argument on behalf of the typological alternative which it illustrates.

Notes

1. For two classic and readily available studies of the milieu of early Christianity with particular attention to pluralism, see Rudolf Bultmann, *Primitive Christianity in its Contemporary Setting*, R. H. Fuller, tr. (Cleveland: World Publishing–Meridian Books, 1956), esp. pp. 135-79; and Arthur Darby Nock, *Early Gentile Christianity and its Hellenistic Background* (New York: Harper & Row–Torchbooks, 1964), esp. pp. 15-23, 35-46, 57-87, 105-45. For more detailed exposition and extensive notes, see Martin P. Nilsson, *Geschichte der griechischen Religion* (Munich: Verlag C. H. Beck, 1950), pp. 48-124, 175-294, 311-76, 555-672. For a recent impressive study which is conversant with relevant literature in contemporary anthropology and sociology, see John G. Gager, *Kingdom and Community: The Social World of Early Christianity* (Englewood Cliffs, N.J.: Prentice-Hall, 1975).
2. Hegel advances this argument repeatedly in numerous forms and in a variety of contexts. Perhaps his most cogent formulation is in the Introduction to the *Phenomenology*. See G. W. F. Hegel, *The Phenomenology of Mind*, J. B. Baillie, tr. (New York: Harper & Row–Torchbooks, 1967), pp. 131-45.
3. In my *Christologies and Cultures: Toward a Typology of Religious Worldviews* (Atlantic Highlands, N.J.: Humanities Press, 1974), I elaborate in considerable detail the alternatives which I only adumbrate here. See esp. chaps. 3, 4, 7, and 10.

II

Zen, Existentialism, and the "Modern" Religious Situation

In assaying the contemporary religious situation, sociologist Robert Bellah's article entitled "Religious Evolution" provides a convenient and useful point of reference. The line of argument which Bellah advances is, to be sure, scarcely a new one. Indeed, his typology may be viewed as little more than a twentieth-century restatement in sociological categories of Hegel's interpretation of the history of culture. But the article does nonetheless afford a concise and sophisticated outline of religious development and thereby establishes a context for interpreting contemporary experience in general and its religious dimension in particular.

Like Hegel, Bellah sees a line of development which, expressed in its most abstract form, is a movement from a monistic religious system through a radical dualism to a rejection of that dualism and hence a reaffirmation of some version of holistic metaphysic. Again like Hegel, Bellah interprets this movement in its psychological, social, and cultural ramifications and not simply as a development confined to a narrowly construed religious sphere. "Religious Evolution" is, in short, a highly compressed outline of the history of human culture. As such, it is as ambitious in its intention as the most speculative of philosophies of history. But Bellah's approach has two undeniable advantages over such predecessors as Hegel. First, his use of the vocabulary and methodology of the social sciences is more generally accessible than the philosophical language of his predecessors. And second, Bellah has the incalculable asset of the historical and systematic data accumulated over the last century.

Bellah's Typology in "Religious Evolution"

Bellah organizes a typology of religious worldviews around what he terms one of "the massive facts of human religious history." That fact is "the emergence in the first millennium B.C. all across the Old World, at least in centers of high culture, of the phenomenon of religious rejection of the world characterized by an extremely negative evaluation of man and society and the exaltation of another realm of reality as alone true and infinitely valuable."[1] Bellah contrasts this religious attitude of world rejection with what he calls "primitive religion" and "modern religion." Although Bellah outlines five types of religious worldview, his line of argument is evident from a comparison of "primitive" and "modern" perspectives with the radical world rejection of what he terms "historic religion." In each case the contrast involves the religious system as a whole—not simply isolated elements within it.

As Bellah summarizes, "primitive religions are on the whole oriented to a single cosmos—they know nothing of a wholly different world relative to which the actual world is utterly devoid of value."[2] Primitive myths exemplify this pattern in that "the mythical world is related to the detailed features of the actual world."[3] Religious action or ritual in turn entails identification with or participation in mythical deeds or events.[4] This investment of concrete life in the present with religious value through myth and ritual has its parallel in the religious organization of "primitive" society: religious organization as a separate social structure does not exist. To use a convenient anachronism, "church and society are one."[5] Hence religious myth, ritual, and organization serve to "reinforce the solidarity of the society" and to "induct the young into the norms of tribal behavior" with the result that "primitive religion gives little leverage from which to change the world."[6]

In contrast to the primitive type, "historic religions" are dualistic. Here again religious beliefs and actions have their correlates in religious organization and its relation to other social structures. "Historic religions" express their dualistic worldview in various ways. The distinction between the natural and the supernatural is an example of a self-consciously conceptual contrast; the difference between this world and life after death illustrates a recurrent popular formulation. But whatever the specific contrast, the effect is a negative valuation of this life in comparison to another realm. Hence the goal of religious action is salvation or release from this world.[7] Bellah argues that one result of this dualism is the emergence of "a clearly structured conception of the self"—"a responsible self, a core self or a true self, deeper than the flux of everyday experience."[8] This view of the self comes to awareness as the correlate of the true reality toward which the self aspires. The same contrast is evident in the social organization of cultures which Bellah describes as historic. In contrast to the fusion of religious life into the social and political organization of "primitive" tribes, there emerge "two at least partially independent hierarchies, one political and one religious."[9] This distinction between the religious organization and the rest of the social order expresses and reinforces the ultimate contrast between the true and real realm and everyday life. The result is that while religion still frequently functions to legitimate the existing social order it also has a new role:

Religion, then, provided the ideology and social cohesion for many rebellions and reform movements in the historic civilizations, and consequently played a more dynamic and especially a more purposive role in social change than had previously been possible.[10]

The difference between the historic type and Bellah's interpretation of "modern religion" may be summarized succinctly: "The central feature of the change is the collapse of the dualism that was crucial to all the historic religions."[11] The implications of this contention are, however, very considerable. Bellah stresses that the modern type is not simply a return to the monism of "primitive" culture:

It is not that a single world has replaced a double one but that an infinitely multiplex one has replaced the simple duplex structure. It is not that life has become again a "one possibility thing" but that it has become an infinite possibility thing.[12]

The radical pluralism of the "modern" religious situation is exemplified not only in the multiplicity of symbol systems but also in the myriad and often conflicting norms for action and the modes of organization through which religious impulses are expressed. Like "primitive" society, the "modern" social order evidences a diffusion of the religious quest throughout the culture. But this diffusion occurs in the context of an unprecedentedly high degree of social differentiation rather than because there are not yet discrete religious organizations. There is a parallel difference in the at least relative world acceptance which Bellah's primitive and modern types share in contrast to the world rejection of "historic religion." Bellah states this difference concisely:

In the earlier world-accepting phases religious conceptions and social order were so fused that it was almost impossible to criticize the latter from the point of view of the former. In the latter phases the possibility of remaking the world to conform to value demands has served in a very different way to mute the extremes of world rejection.[13]

For the modern type, acceptance of this world is, then, an acceptance which includes a recognition of the possibility of changing (and therefore the responsibility to change) that world—not a resignation to the unalterable.

The Primitive and Historic Types Today

In "Religious Evolution" Bellah on occasion suggests that his typology delineates a process through which religious worldviews succeed each other and render antecedent types obsolete. In discussing the modern type, for example, he notes that "the dualistic worldview certainly persists in the minds of many of the devout."[14] But this persistence is at least implicitly viewed as the result of a cultural lag—as an inappropriate vestige of an earlier era. Hence he can state that "in the worldview that has emerged from the tremendous intellectual advances of the last two centuries there is simply no room for a hierarchic dualistic religious symbol system of the classical historic type."[15] Since he wrote that article (1964) Bellah has, however, indicated that he considers preceding types to be continuing alternatives in each of the subsequent stages, including the "modern" one. This change in emphasis is, I think, worth exploring.[16]

The discussion in "Religious Evolution" does specify the existence of multiple perspectives as a salient feature of the "modern" situation:

The fundamental symbolization of modern man and his situation is that of a dynamic multi-dimensional self capable, within limits, of continual self-transformation and capable, again within limits, of remaking the world including the very symbolic forms with which he deals with it.[17]

In discussing this growing awareness among contemporary people of their responsibility for the symbol systems they choose, Bellah also indicates that he expects the maintenance of traditional religious symbolism as well as its development in new directions:

I expect traditional religious symbolism to be maintained and developed in new directions, but with growing awareness that it is symbolism and that man in the last analysis is responsible for the choice of his symbolism.[18]

But despite this recognition of radical pluralism in the contemporary religious situation—pluralism inclusive of traditional symbolism—the line of argument in "Religious Evolution" does not seem to allow for and certainly does not emphasize the continued viability of the primitive or the historic types in their traditional forms as religious world-views for "modern" people.

In contrast to this suggestion of a linear succession of types stands Bellah's awareness of the extent to which "primitive" and "historic" symbolism is very attractive to and therefore powerful in cultural contexts which otherwise seem to correlate with his own outline of the "modern" situation. Perhaps the most imposing illustration of this apparent paradox is Norman O. Brown's *Love's Body*, which Bellah reviewed appreciatively in 1969.[19] In his introduction to *Beyond Belief*, Bellah addresses this complex of issues explicitly, though only in passing. In a footnote he writes:

This is one of the characteristics of stage five [the modern type]—that within it everything previous may have direct meaning. . . . Indeed some of the most "primitive" levels of religious experience, the direct participation in myth and symbol, may be especially characteristic of religion in stage five.[20]

And, in a more personal statement, he records his own experience as an example of a "modern" man who re-appropriates traditional symbolism:

For the deepest truth I have discovered is that if one accepts the loss, if one gives up clinging to what is irretrievably gone, then the nothing which is left is not barren but enormously fruitful. Everything that one has lost comes flooding back again out of the darkness, and one's relation to it is new—free and unclinging.[21]

Important as is the observation that traditional symbolism may be a powerful force in contemporary religious life, it should not, however, obscure the accuracy of Bellah's contention in "Religious Evolution" that self-consciously "modern" people cannot simply affirm "primitive" or "historic" symbol systems in their classic or traditional forms. For traditional symbolism affirmed self-consciously as compatible with "modernity" is not simply a restatement of "primitive" or "historic" religion. Instead it entails at least an implicit conceptual and imaginative translation into the "modern" situation of cultural pluralism combined with the collapse of any ultimate metaphysical dualism.

The "Modern" Situation and the Question of God

To specify this often implicit process of translation, it is, I think, helpful to outline the multiple possible "modern" responses to a perennial religious question—and to observe how those responses are and are not the same as those of "primitive" and "historic" religion. The question which in my judgment allows for a systematic differentiation of alternative responses is the equivalent, for the post-Enlightenment West, of the traditional question as to the existence of God. Insofar as the experience of the post-Enlightenment West entails the collapse of traditional metaphysical dualisms, this question cannot, however, refer to the existence or nonexistence of a being or entity beyond the world. Instead the question of God becomes, more or less self-consciously, a query as to the character of the cosmos—the nature of the self's ultimate environment.

That there is this change in the reference of the God question follows without further argument if one accept Bellah's description of the modern type as characteristic of the post-Enlightenment West. But it still may be useful to survey the line of historical development which acceptance of Bellah's description presupposes.

In both Judaism and Christianity there has always been a persistent emphasis on the significance and value of life in this world. Commitment to a view of the world as the divine creation and celebration of deliverance from bondage in Egypt may serve to epitomize the centrality of this emphasis. The result is that sharply dualistic tendencies in the Judeo-Christian tradition—Jewish apocalypticism and the eschatological emphasis in early Christianity, for example—stand in tension with an underlying commitment to the value of earthly existence. In the development of Christian doctrine, this positive valuation of life finds further dramatic expression through the dogma that, in the person and work of Christ, God is present and active in the world. When the church is seen as in some sense the continuation of this divine incarnation, the positive appraisal of earthly life is, moreover, formulated in terms important for concrete social and institutional life. Yet despite this emphasis on the at least potential goodness of the created order, there is still in most forms of traditional Jewish and Christian piety and theology an affirmation of another reality superior to life in space and time. Significant as the created order may be, it is interpreted as grounded in a transcendent reality in comparison with which it is emphatically deficient, inadequate, fallen. And that other reality—the true, the good, the fully real—is the ultimate goal of the religious life.

That other reality is, of course, what the experience of the West from the Enlightenment on has rendered more and more problematical. Already in the eighteenth century the world view of Newtonian physics seemed to many intellectuals to preclude at least the popular images of heavenly fulfillment for the faithful and of an all-powerful transcendent being who intervened at will in the causal order. Consistent materialism and atheism were, to be sure, still the exception even among intellectuals. Newton himself, for example, was interested in speculative theology and considered himself to be a Christian. But the conceptual difficulties in affirming a transcendent divine being and survival in another realm after death became increasingly critical. By the end of the Enlightenment the writings of even many of those who sought to defend traditional commitments give evidence of the new situation.

Perhaps the most instructive and certainly the most influential example of this change is Kant's philosophy. After analyzing what is presupposed about human knowing if Newtonian physics is accepted as valid, Kant attempted to specify the conditions which are assumed or postulated in moral action. The result of this analysis of human ac-

tion was for Kant that persons postulate the existence of human freedom, of God, and of immortality whenever they act. There are some
problems with Kant's position, particularly his somewhat uncritical
assumption that the specific western symbols "God" and "immortality" must be postulated. But Kant's line of argument is in any case
symptomatic of the post-Enlightenment western situation insofar as it
begins with life in space and time and then postulates what is required to make significant human action possible. Kant's rational
faith in God and immortality is, in short, the expression of confidence
that humanity's ultimate environment is conducive to and supportive
of moral action. As I have indicated in discussing the epistemological
presuppositions of dogmatism and unqualified relativism, Kant maintains that nothing can be known (in his technical sense of observing
or speculative or theoretical knowledge) about God and immortality;
but insofar as people act morally they at least implicitly affirm or postulate this ultimate context of meaning for their action.

The dominant cultural tendencies of the nineteenth and twentieth centuries have not reversed the order of argument which Kant
illustrates. Accordingly, religious affirmations have typically been intimately related to interpreting life in this world. Friedrich Schleiermacher, the most influential of post-Reformation Protestant theologians, formulates this position in systematic form when he describes
Christian doctrines as interpretations or accounts of the Christian religious self-consciousness. Many religious thinkers have no doubt
opposed Schleiermacher's theological approach. That Karl Barth is
among the opponents demonstrates that they are not simply minor or
peripheral figures. But the theological method which Schleiermacher
specifies has nonetheless become the dominant approach among religious thinkers of all but the most conservative western traditions. The
result is that whatever has been affirmed about God—to focus again
on this paradigmatic example of belief—has with increasing self-
consciousness been recognized as a symbolic interpretation or expression of the ultimate conditions of human experience.

The Systematic Alternatives

The equivalent in the "modern" situation of the traditional question
of the existence of God is, then, the query as to the nature or character of the self's ultimate environment conceived as continuous with

life in the present rather than as another reality complete and perfect apart from the world. This reformulation of the question does not in itself entail denial of the transcendence of the divine or the ultimate. It requires only that transcendence as interpreted in the metaphysical dualism of "historic religion" be reconceived. Indeed, in its form as addressing the nature or character of the self's ultimate environment, the question of transcendence continues to be raised at least implicitly even when explicitly theological or religious issues are not under consideration. Consequently, attention to the possible responses to this form of the God question affords the promise not only of differentiating among alternative contemporary religious positions but also of focusing systematic parallels between religious and ostensibly non-religious perspectives.

The question of the nature of this ultimate environment becomes more focused if it is addressed from the perspective of its relation to human activity. When the question is so formulated, the various responses may be classified with reference to four systematically distinct positions. The first is little more than a limiting case. It is that the universe is so constituted as utterly to frustrate all human action. Not only is there no cosmic support for human efforts, but those efforts themselves have no hope of realization. This alternative is, in short, an uncompromising nihilism. The second response is the radical opposite of this first one. It affirms all that is. Hence human existence is ingredient in a totality which need only be rightly apprehended to be appreciated without qualification. This alternative is exemplified in Zen Buddhism, but as a type it certainly is not confined to that particular tradition. The third possible response is to view human agents as struggling in a neutral or indifferent universe, but struggling with the prospect of realizing limited though still significant goals. This perspective is expressed in much of the literature and philosophy of existentialism. The fourth response shares with existentialism an emphasis on the creative power of human action, but it combines this emphasis with an ultimately positive appraisal of the cosmos, an appraisal which affirms what is as in the process of becoming good even though that potential is not yet fully actualized. Like the second and third alternatives, this fourth one is exemplified in many philosophical, religious, and quasi-religious traditions. But the philosophy of Hegel is in my view an exceptionally incisive and provocative articulation of this position.[22]

The differences among the four positions are evident in their distinguishable approaches to the question of transcendence. Nihilism by definition asserts that there is no meaning or value—transcendent or otherwise. But the other three positions may be construed as representing attempts to reconceive transcendence as it is interpreted in the metaphysical dualism of "historic religion." For the Zen type, transcendence assumes the form of attaining a human perspective radically different from that of ordinary experience—a perspective from which the truth of the whole of reality becomes visible. It is in effect an epistemological transcendence. In the existentialist type, critical distance from the everyday is expressed through individual authenticity as opposed to social conformism. It is an ethical transcendence that sets the true mode of human orientation and action over against its trivialization in conventional life. Finally, in the Hegelian type, transcendence is affirmed in the tension between the actual and the ideal, the already attained and the ultimate goal. It is a historical transcendence that calls into question every present state of affairs through reference to the ideal or ultimate end that is its destiny.

I do not intend to explore the first response in any detail because I view unqualified nihilism as an untenable philosophy in the literal sense that no one holds to it. That people continue to live is itself an implicit denial of total nihilism. And even suicide is an act which at the least affirms its own significance. Each of the other three responses is, however, an important and frequently maintained position. Each of them is, moreover, represented in eastern as well as in western cultures and in religious as well as ostensibly nonreligious forms. Consequently the Zen, the existentialist, and the Hegelian types invite further attention—the first two briefly in the remainder of this chapter and the third in more detail in the next chapter.

It should perhaps be stated explicitly that responses to a question like that of the nature or character of the self's ultimate environment are not simply intellectual or theoretical answers. Responses are in any case conditioned by the social communities and cultural traditions in which a person participates. But responses are also inseparable from the individual's personal development. Erik Erikson has analyzed the interdependence of religious affirmation and psychological dynamics very perceptively in the cases of such imposing figures as Luther and Gandhi. Critics of Erikson's approach may prefer a frame of reference other than his broadly psychoanalytic one or may disagree with his specific execution of his own program. There is, however, no disputing that, for Luther and Gandhi and everyone else, responses to religious questions are related to such psychological dynamics as having/not having what Erikson terms "basic trust" or developing/not developing a sense of autonomy.

I want to underscore my recognition of the importance of personal, social, and cultural conditioning so as to avoid a possible misunderstanding of the argument I am advancing. The types which I outline are ideal types in the sense in which Max Weber and social scientists under his influence (Robert Bellah, for example) use the term. They are, in short, heuristic constructs which serve to organize empirical data—though, in contrast to those social scientists who claim to employ only descriptive types, I attempt to develop a classification which I see as in principle exhaustive. As I have indicated in my remarks on theological method, I consider this systematizing of alternatives which usually remain only implicitly or inchoately distinguished to be helpful in appraising particular worldviews, including my own. And, as will become increasingly evident, the typology which I develop also serves as a vehicle for commending the perspective which I judge to be the most adequate. I do not, however, want to be understood as suggesting that the religious life is simply a process of rational selection among the abstract types resulting from my systematic analysis. Though I do not pretend to explore all of the complex personal, social, and cultural dynamics through which the worldviews of individuals and communities are shaped, I nonetheless presuppose the crucial role which those dynamics play even while I deliberately abstract from them in order to outline the types which I am proposing.

The Zen Type

The type which Zen represents is a recurrent tendency in the history of religions—especially in the East, but also in the West. Indeed, it is sometimes advanced as the central commitment of religion as such. Among those maintaining this position is D. T. Suzuki, the first prominent Asian interpreter of Zen to the West. In a particularly striking passage he writes:

Whatever we may say about moral ideals of perfection, religion is after all the acceptance of things as they are, things evil together with things good.

. . . "You are all right as you are," or "to be well with God and the world," or "don't think of the morrow"—this is the final word of all religion. . . . To strive, which means to "negate," is, according to Buddhist phraseology, eternally to transmigrate in the ocean of birth and death.[23]

In my judgment it is an arbitrary narrowing of religion to restrict it to this one perspective. But Suzuki is right in stressing the prominence in the history of religions of this affirmation of what is. In the language of Zen or of its philosophical antecedents, the Mādhyamika and Yogācārin schools of Mahāyāna Buddhism, everyone and everything is Buddha-nature, saṃsāra is nirvāṇa, phenomenal existence is ultimate reality. Zen is no doubt the best known representative of this position in recent years in the West. An earlier generation was, however, attracted to a similarly systematic and uncompromising form of the same position as expressed in the Advaita Vedānta of Hinduism. And for significant circles of intellectuals, the philosophies of such westerners as Spinoza and Bradley have articulated the same interpretation of the whole of reality as eternally perfect and complete.

Especially in its religious forms, this type of worldview does not encourage or result in passive resignation. Indeed, Zen in particular is well known for its elaborate and intensive programs of disciplined religious practice. This practice is, however, designed to effect a transformation in the disciples' point of view so that they perceive phenomenal existence (saṃsāra) to be already and always identical with ultimate reality (nirvāṇa). T. R. V. Murti, writing on Nāgārjuna and the Mādhyamika school (which he views as central to the development of Mahāyāna Buddhism and which is in any case an important historical influence on Zen), registers this contention very emphatically:

Nirvana, says Nagarjuna, is non-ceasing, unachieved. There is only the dissolution of false views (kalpanaksaya), but no becoming in the real. . . . There is only change in our outlook, not in reality. . . . The function of prajna [wisdom] is not to transform the real, but only to create a change in our attitude towards it. The change is epistemic (subjective), not ontological (objective). The real is as it has ever been.[24]

The sharp distinction which Murti draws between epistemological and ontological change is, I think, problematical on the idealist premises which inform this whole tradition. For on those premises, a change in consciousness is also a change in the real. His use of the distinction is, however, illuminating even if it is overstated because it may serve to focus the similarities and differences between Zen and the primitive type that Bellah outlines.

There are significant parallels. Like "primitive religion," Zen is oriented to a single cosmos. Accordingly, both types emphasize present experience and see it as significant in itself—as participating in the real. But there are also profound differences. Perhaps the most instructive is that, in contrast to "primitive religion," Zen and those perspectives like it have some variant on a two-truths theory of knowledge. To ordinary perception, reality is differentiated into particulars and appears to be less than perfect. But to true insight or wisdom, all of reality is seen to be an undifferentiated and fully realized unity. Hence everyday empirical knowledge is illusory—though it may have its provisional uses. This double epistemology is, of course, employed to refute the contention of "historic religion" that this world is radically deficient in comparison to ultimate transcendent reality. Precisely in denying every such ultimate metaphysical dualism, the type which Zen represents must, however, be distinguished from "primitive religion." For in that very denial, Zen presupposes the crucial importance of an issue with which the primitive type scarcely concerns itself. Zen is, in short, the reaffirmation of a monistic position over against a dualistic perspective, whereas "primitive religion" is unaware of those two positions as competing alternatives and as a result does not appeal to a systematically articulated doctrine of two truths.

Zen and Existentialism: A Contrast in Types

Existentialism as a type of response to the "modern" situation stands in sharp contrast to the position which Zen represents. Zen teaches that the self is at home in the universe, that the individual is finally at one with an encompassing and undifferentiated reality. In contrast, existentialism emphasizes the antagonism between persons and their environments, the need for individuals to stand over against their society and culture and even nature itself. Each position has its at least implicit ontology. For Zen the individual is in the last analysis not an independent entity. Whatever reality individuals have is derivative from their union with the whole. Existentialism reverses this setting of ontological priorities. The status of all universals is problematical. But the particular existing individual is unquestionably real.

This ontological contrast between emphasis on union with the whole on the one hand and the unique and autonomous individual's experience of conflict on the other is reflected in the epistemological views on the limits of human knowing characteristic of the two types. In explicating its doctrine of two truths Zen allows that the conceptuality of language is useful for ordinary empirical knowledge with its (ultimately false) differentiation of particulars within the universe. It insists, however, that language is fundamentally misleading if it is employed in an attempt to know or describe the unitary whole which is ultimate reality. An existentialist like Kierkegaard also emphasizes the limitations of language. But for him conceptions are universal terms which are inadequate and false only when they tempt their users into the delusion that general descriptions or propositions can grasp existing individuals in their particular concreteness. Both traditions insist on the final poverty of conceptions. But the focus of the argument is in each case on what for that tradition is of ultimate significance: the whole of being for Zen, the existing individual for existentialism.

Differences in ontological and epistemological commitments are not, of course, without ethical and religious implications. Perhaps the most succinct way to approach those implications is to refer again to Bellah's typology and the question of transcendence. While the Zen acceptance and even affirmation of the universe as it is indicates systematic common ground with "primitive religion," this shared position in turn provides a vivid contrast to the ethical stance of existentialism. At the same time, its restless dissatisfaction with what is, its stance over against not only existing societies and cultures but even the cosmos itself, represents an intriguing systematic parallel between the existentialist type and "historic religion." Like Zen, existentialism rejects the metaphysical dualism of "historic religion." Again like Zen, existentialism develops an alternative dualism to express transcendence of the everyday or the ordinary. But while Zen elaborates an epistemological doctrine of two truths which allows it to account for the apparent deficiencies of phenomenal existence, existentialism advocates an apprehension of the world that emphasizes division along ethical lines. Though existentialism knows only this world, it bifurcates that one reality into the light of authenticity and the much more widespread darkness of inauthenticity. The result is that while the epistemological dualism of Zen enables it to accept the whole of reality despite appearances, the ethical dualism of existentialism continues the differentiation into two opposed realms characteristic of "historic religion."

That existentialism and Zen may be contrasted in their respective ontologies, epistemologies, and ethics is, of course, a consequence of their reflecting and interpreting different ranges of human experience. To indulge in psychoanalytic reductionism, Zen is oral and existentialism is anal. Though Zen Buddhists insist on the impossibility of capturing the truth of *nirvāṇa* in language, they still talk and write about it. And their reflections on Zen practice agree that, whatever else Enlightenment may mean, it involves an experience of belonging inclusion in or union with the whole of reality. One result of this experience is an appreciation of every detail of even the apparently most mundane of actions or occurrences. Hence Zen insists that total involvement in viewing a flower or in releasing an arrow from a bow or in washing dishes may all alike be vehicles for expressing the truth that everything is Buddha-nature. In contrast to Zen's nonjudgmental acceptance, existentialism is inherently critical even when it maintains, as Heidegger does in *Being and Time,* that it is only describing and not making value judgments, or when it argues, as Sartre at least halfheartedly does in *Being and Nothingness,* that the specific projects a person undertakes are finally a matter of indifference. To use the categories which may be traced as a *Leitmotif* all through Heidegger's *Being and Time,* there is a fundamental opposition between the person whose living authentically testifies to his irreducible individuality (*Jemeinigkeit*) and the mass of people who simply and inauthentically exist in the impersonality of everyday life. This dichotomized vision generalizes a range of experiences clearly different from the mystical union of Zen. It is the experience of opposition, of establishing an autonomous identity over against a culture which is described as inauthentic or unfree even while claiming that no value judgments are implied. It is, in short, an experience similar in its psychological dynamics to that of "historic religion's" rejection of this world in favor of a perfect transcendent realm.

Existentialism—the Type and the
Historical Movement

In outlining the existentialist type of response to the "modern" religious situation, I have focused my exposition through contrasts with Zen so as to indicate the contours of what I see as two contrasted ideal types. The existentialist type as I outline it is not accurate in every detail for all those thinkers frequently included in the rubric "existentialism." I maintain that it is, however, representative of at least one central tradition within this movement.

Existentialism as a nineteenth- and twentieth-century movement was and is nurtured by profound disenchantment with western culture. That attitude was already powerfully evident in such nineteenth-century figures as Kierkegaard, Nietzsche, and Dostoevski. But only in this century has thorough disenchantment become a pervasive cultural mood, particularly in Germany after World War I and in France during and after World War II. That mood is poignantly expressed in the literature of the era. To note only four literary figures representative of different genres: Rainer Maria Rilke in his poetry, Franz Kafka in his short stories and novels, Albert Camus in his philosophical essays and novels, and Samuel Beckett in his drama all register and in turn evoke what may in a general sense be termed an existentialist pathos with the human situation as twentieth-century people experience it. Despite the power and the influence of artistic portrayal, however, "existentialism" is more usually reserved for the thinkers who have interpreted the same mood self-consciously as philosophers. Who those philosophers are is itself a complicated question, since each of the most influential ones, except for Sartre, has explicitly disowned the name. But in addition to Sartre, the designation invariably also includes Jaspers and Heidegger. Although they have been less influential, the religious existentialists Gabriel Marcel and Rudolf Bultmann are frequently included as well.

Because I consider them to be the philosophers most representative of existentialism as a broader cultural movement, I have modeled my description of the existentialist type on the positions of the early Heidegger and Sartre. I have, however, generalized the existentialist type so that it conforms to the position reflected in the movement as a whole even if the resultant description conflicts with a specific line of argument developed in one or another of Heidegger's or Sartre's writings. There are two instances of this generalizing procedure which I have already adumbrated but which require further comment.

The first is that I do not confine the existentialist type to those thinkers who, like Heidegger, contend that their description is value free. Although existentialism is not infrequently allied with what purports to be a strictly descriptive phenomenological method, there seems to me to be no necessary connection between existentialism and claims for value-free analysis.

The second instance of my generalizing the type rather than following one specific position has to do with a closely related issue in Sartre's *Being and Nothingness*. In the closing pages of that work Sartre asserts "that all human activities are equivalent . . . and that all are on principle doomed to failure." He sums up with an aphorism: "Thus it amounts to the same thing whether one gets drunk or is a leader of nations."[25] This starkly relativistic and finally nihilistic conclusion is not simply a rhetorical flourish. Indeed, it is arguable that despite Sartre's own attempt in the final paragraph of the book to hold out the hope of a solution to this dilemma, the position systematically implied in the ontology of *Being and Nothingness* is a consistent nihilism.[26] Even if that judgment is correct, it does not, however, seem to me to furnish an adequate ground for restricting existentialism as a type to this position. Significantly, Sartre himself attempts to avoid the nihilistic conclusion which his "phenomenological ontology" seems to imply. In this sense Sartre's own political activism, much of his literary work, the elaboration of his existential psychoanalysis, such popular lectures as "Existentialism is a Humanism," and his turn to Marxism all represent a continuation of the efforts suggested in the final paragraph of *Being and Nothingness* —even though the systematic ethical work promised there was never written. This combination of efforts may not succeed in systematically rethinking the ontology which in *Being and Nothingness* results in apparent nihilism. But the influence which this later work has exercised is nonetheless a further argument against restricting existentialism as a type to every conclusion of Sartre's early work.

Existentialism and Zen as Complementary Types

A third distinction between existentialism as a general type and the positions of particular thinkers is more directly relevant to the line of argument of this study. It concerns Heidegger rather than Sartre. In delineating the contrast with Zen, I have deliberately concentrated on the individualistic strain in existentialism. Especially in Heidegger's later thought, there is, however, also an emphasis on the question of being as such, which has definite affinities not only with some expressions of Christian mysticism but also with Zen. Enthusiasts for both traditions in the East as well as the West have frequently noted the parallels. Despite my distinction between the individualistic and the holistic motifs, I do not want to deny either the existence or the importance of their mutual affinities. I do, however, want to focus attention on their very different, even if complementary, strengths.

The Zen and the existentialist types as I have outlined them represent the contrasting strengths of the individualistic and the holistic motifs. The virtue of the existentialist type is its programmatically critical stance. Its dichotomized perspective facilitates judgments about what it perceives to be inadequacies in personal, social, and cultural life. In this role, it is the heir to those traditions which set themselves over against established conventions and institutions in the name of a more authentic mode of existence, however it may be interpreted. The strength of the Zen position seems at first to be simply the opposite of this tendency to evaluate and if need be appraise negatively. For that strength is its positive valuation of the whole of being and, consequently, its appreciative awareness of the details of every action and occurrence. Zen does, to be sure, resist this use of evaluative categories. But even in speaking of the emptiness or suchness of all things, Zen at the same time affirms this emptiness or suchness—an affirmation perhaps more evident in its willingness to substitute "Buddha-nature" and its equivalents for "emptiness" or "suchness."

It is significant and exciting that there are interpretations of both Zen and existentialism that seek to combine the strengths represented in the two types so as to fuse their respective holistic and individualistic emphases. Insofar as such interpretations continue to share the premises of either Zen or existentialism, they are, however, systematically opposed to another approach that also attempts to integrate the two sets of virtues but on different premises. To this alternative to existentialism and Zen I now turn.

Notes

1. Robert Bellah, "Religious Evolution," in *Reader in Comparative Religion: An Anthropological Approach,* W. A. Lessa and E. Z. Vogt, eds. (New York: Harper & Row, 1965), p. 74. This article is also available (with more detailed documentation) in Bellah, *Beyond Belief: Essays on Religion in a Post-Traditional World* (New York: Harper & Row, 1970), pp. 20-50. The parallel passage is on p. 22. In subsequent references to this article, the parenthetical page number indicates the same passage in *Beyond Belief.*
2. "Religious Evolution," p. 75 (23).
3. Ibid. p. 77 (27).
4. Ibid. p. 77-78 (28).
5. Ibid. p. 78 (28).
6. Ibid. p. 78 (29).
7. Ibid. p. 80 (32-33).
8. Ibid. pp. 80-81 (33-34). *See also* p. 87 (45).
9. Ibid. p. 81 (34).
10. Ibid. p. 82 (35-36).
11. Ibid. p. 84 (40).
12. Ibid. p. 84 (40).
13. Ibid. p. 87 (45).
14. Ibid. p. 85 (41-42).
15. Ibid. p. 84 (40).
16. I have in mind here a particular discussion with Bellah at Harvard's Center for the Study of World Religions in fall 1970 in which he was explicit on this point.
17. "Religious Evolution," p. 85 (42).
18. Ibid. p. 85 (42).
19. This review is included in *Beyond Belief,* pp. 230-36.
20. *Beyond Belief,* p. xxii.
21. Ibid. pp. xx-xxi.
22. This typology is continuous with the more complex set of distinctions I develop in my *Christologies and Cultures: Toward a Typology of Religious Worldviews* (Atlantic Highlands, N.J.: Humanities Press, 1974). As I will indicate in some detail in the next chapter, there are also parallels between the types I propose and systematic patterns in the thought of such philosophers as Peirce and Hegel. Of more recent thinkers, the person who has influenced me most directly is Wayne Proudfoot of Columbia University. Over a period of ten years of frequent discussion, his remarkable gifts of analysis and argument have been a continuing source of stimulation and insight. For his own systematization of a closely related set of issues, see his *God and the Self: Three Types of Philosophy of Religion* (Lewisburg, Pa.: Bucknell University Press, 1976).

23. D. T. Suzuki, *Essays in Zen Buddhism, Second Series* (London: Rider, 1958), p. 283.
24. T. R. V. Murti, *The Central Philosophy of Buddhism* (London: George Allen and Unwin, 1960), pp. 233, 273-74. For less technically philosophical statements of the same point in a variety of contexts (respected traditional sermons and letters, contemporary lectures and interviews), see Philip Kaplean (ed.), *Three Pillars of Zen* (Boston: Beacon Press, 1967), pp. 54-57, 77, 80, 116, 120, 160-61, 166-67, 173, 232, 249-50, 267-68. Similar references to other books on Zen could of course be multiplied indefinitely.
25. Jean-Paul Sartre, *Being and Nothingness: An Essay on Phenomenological Ontology*, H. E. Barnes, tr. (New York: Philosophical Library, 1956), p. 627.
26. For a concise exploration of this complex of issues, see Richard J. Bernstein, *Praxis and Action* (Philadelphia: University of Pennsylvania Press, 1971), pp. 122-64, esp. 142, 148-64.

III

The Alternative to
Existentialism and Zen

To speak of the alternative to existentialism and Zen cannot but appear to be an extravagant indulgence in arrogance. If the foregoing analysis of the "modern" religious situation is correct, there have been, however, only two systematic alternatives to existentialism and Zen since the collapse of "historic" dualism. And because a consistent nihilism seems to me to be only a hypothetical limiting case, there is in fact only one position remaining. It is the perspective which not only affirms with existentialism that constructive human action to create meaning and value is possible but also agrees with Zen that the self's ultimate environment is hospitable toward or supportive of this activity. The parallel seems at first to be especially marked in the case of Zen. The difference between the two positions may, however, be expressed succinctly in Buddhist terminology. While Zen insists that life just as it is in space and time (*saṃsāra*) is in truth ultimate reality (*nirvāṇa*), this third alternative maintains that *saṃsāra* has the potential to become *nirvāṇa*, or that *nirvāṇa* is the destiny of *saṃsāra*. The third position is, then, radically processive in that it sees value being realized not only through individual human action but also through ongoing natural and cultural development. New insight or vision and critical judgment or opposition are, in short, integrated into transcendence historically conceived.

The Philosophy of Peirce and the
Need for Thirdness

One approach to establishing the differences between Zen and existentialism on the one hand and the alternative to them on the other is through the thought of Charles Sanders Pierce, the provocative American philosopher. Peirce elaborates a categorial scheme and employs it throughout his writings to illuminate the most disparate of topics. The scheme is superficially very simple, in that it consists of only three categories: Firstness, Secondness, and Thirdness. Yet Peirce maintains both that all three of his categories are necessary to explain even a single phenomenon and that the three taken together are sufficient to systematize or categorize the whole of human experience. Whatever its intrinsic merits—and I think they are considerable —the scheme is of interest for the line of argument I am advancing because of the correlation between Peirce's categories and the emphases characteristic of Zen, existentialism, and what I consider the more adequate alternative to them. Accordingly, his categories may serve to epitomize the distinctions among the three positions.

Peirce uses the category "Firstness" to designate "the unanalyzed total impression made by any manifold not thought of as actual fact, but simply as quality, as simple positive possibility of appearance."[1] The crucial characteristic of Firstness is, then, immediacy: it is a total impression which is neither analyzed nor related to other impressions. There is, accordingly, no temporal mediation in Firstness:

The immediate present, could we seize it, would have no character but its Firstness. Not that I mean to say that immediate consciousness (a pure fiction, by the way) would be Firstness, but that the *quality* of what we are immediately conscious of, which is no fiction, is Firstness.[2]

Among Peirce's innumerable examples of Firstness, one concise list suggests the range of possibilities: "a vague, unobjectified, still less unsubjectified, sense of redness, or of salt taste, or of an ache, or of grief or joy, or of a prolonged musical note."[3] Although Peirce typically focuses his discussion of Firstness through descriptions of direct awareness or feeling, he also terms it a metaphysical category. It then refers to a "monad"—"a pure nature, or quality, in itself without parts of features, and without embodiment."[4] To quote Peirce's own formal definition:

Firstness is the mode of being of that which is such as it is, positively and without reference to anything else.[5]

As a category, Firstness is, of course, an abstraction. But Peirce uses this abstraction to refer to an impression which is irreducibly concrete in the sense that it is a discrete quality unrelated in its immediacy to other aspects of experience.

In contrast to the focus of Firstness on a distinctive and at least provisionally isolated quality, Secondness as a category refers to the experience of duality—*"not mere twoness but active oppugnancy."*[6] Peirce again offers his own vivid illustration:

You get this kind of consciousness in some approach to purity when you put your shoulder against a door and try to force it open. You have a sense of resistance and at the same time a sense of effort. . . . It is a double consciousness. . . . The idea of other, of *not*, becomes a very pivot of thought.[7]

Secondness is, then, an awareness of over againstness. It of course includes dramatic experiences involving a sense of struggle or opposition. But it is also evident in the self's everyday consciousness of itself as distinct from an object or another self. Indeed, Peirce correlates everything which he would designate as "experience" with Secondness because "experience generally is what the course of life has compelled me to think."[8]

The reference of Thirdness is more difficult to specify than is that of Firstness or Secondness. In part, the difficulty is a function of increasing complexity. Whereas Firstness involves a single or monadic quality and Secondness is dyadic in structure, Thirdness describes a triadic relation. The result is that Thirdness necessarily entails mediation, in contrast to the emphasis on immediate awareness or direct experience in Firstness and Secondness. That is, Thirdness refers to forms of experience which presuppose a context of meaning beyond the specific qualities or interactions involved. Hence conventions of all kinds exemplify Thirdness: concepts, signs, laws, norms, habits, and so on. Peirce uses the giving of a present from one person to another as an illustration of Thirdness:

Take, for example, the relation of *giving*. A *gives* B to C. This does not consist of A's throwing B away and its accidentally hitting C, like the date-stone, which hit the Jinnee in the eye. If that were all, it would not be a genuine triadic relation, but merely one dyadic relation followed by another. There need be no motion of the thing given. Giving is a transfer of the right of property. Now right is a matter of law, and law is a matter of thought and meaning.[9]

Also illustrative of Thirdness is the making of a contract. Peirce insists that what is crucial in the process of contracting is not the actual signing of a document but rather the intent which commits the parties to govern their conduct according to "certain conditional rules."[10] Thirdness is, then, the process of mediation through which thought or intention is related to a specific object or person or situation so as to interpret it. Every form of symbolic representation accordingly entails Thirdness:

Representation necessarily involves a genuine triad. For it involves a sign, or representation, of some kind, outward or inward, mediating between an object and an interpreting thought.[11]

Peirce is convinced that every person's experience includes Firstness, Secondness, and Thirdness. Consequently he insists that any philosophical system must, to be adequate, attend to all three categories. He is, however, aware that this requirement is not always met:

Yet I see a great many thinkers who are trying to construct a system without putting any Thirdness into it. Among them are some of my best friends who acknowledge themselves indebted to me for ideas but have never learned the principal lesson.[12]

To borrow Peirce's pedagogical metaphor, this same principal lesson is one which existentialism and Zen have failed to learn.

Zen, Existentialism, and the Question of Mediation

It is, I think, instructive to interpret Zen from the perspective of Peirce's categories. In this context, the Zen type emerges as the elaboration of a total, if often implicit, worldview from the mode of immediate awareness characteristic of Firstness. Peirce himself maintains that Firstness is an abstraction: for him immediate consciousness is, as he observes parenthetically in an already quoted passage, a "pure fiction." But he nonetheless sees it as a useful abstraction for referring to the quality of consciousness which is not in any way conceptually mediated. Because Zen takes the direct insight or awareness of Enlightenment to be normative, it in effect reverses Peirce's judgment. It takes direct and unmediated awareness simply of suchness to be ultimately true and the differentiated and mediated consciousness of everyday experience to be falsely particularized in part at least because of the misleading influence of language. Peirce himself does, of course, refer to specific qualities—the impression of a musical note, the taste of salt, the feeling of joy, and so on. But because Zen completely generalizes the insight of Enlightenment, all such particular qualities are apprehended as partial aspects of what ultimately is the completely unmediated awareness of suchness or the universal Buddha-nature.

The result of this concentration on Firstness is a systematic relegation of concern with social and cultural processes to the status of the less than true or real. For, in contrast to what Zen takes to be the ultimate truth of the human situation, those processes entail differentiation in space and mediation over time. Zen does not, of course, avoid the necessity of relating to social and cultural life. It does, to take the most fundamental example, use language in presenting its position. And it also has had a tremendous influence on Oriental cultures, ranging from painting, poetry, and flower arranging to athletics and military discipline. Even this relation to social and cultural processes is, however, indicative of Zen's focus on Firstness. Though it unavoidably uses words to attempt to communicate its perspective, Zen at the same time prescribes a discipline designed to overcome what it views as the limitations of language so that direct and unmediated awareness becomes possible. Similarly, Zen's influence on Chinese and Japanese cultures is consistent with its systematic commitment to the ultimacy of the immediate and the undifferentiated. If that influence derived from a self-conscious articulation of a role as appraiser of the direction of historical developments, it would be difficult to reconcile with Zen's other commitments. But Zen does not see itself in this critical role. Instead it views itself as simply testifying to the presence of Buddha-nature in all of life as it is.

Just as Zen may be correlated with Peirce's category of Firstness, existentialism may be viewed as a worldview generalized from the mode of experience which he designates as Secondness. That the experience of opposition or polarity or over againstness underlies the existentialist type as I have outlined it need not be belabored. Its emphasis on Secondness and the "active oppugnancy" which it entails is, moreover, what distinguishes existentialism from Zen. Illustrative of the contrast to Zen involved in this emphasis is the critical role which existentialism plays in relation to the conventions of contemporary culture. Also exemplifying this contrast is the aggressive stance which existentialism displays toward nature when it insists that, because the cosmos has no inherent meaning or value, persons cannot simply affirm what is but must first actively create what may then in some limited sense be affirmed. Yet in spite of the contrast between the Zen concern with Firstness and the existentialist focus on Secondness, both traditions agree in declining to interpret human social and cultural life as ultimately significant. The approaches to this negative agreement are, to be sure, very different. Whereas Zen finally dissolves the apparent person into an encompassing whole, existentialism exalts the autonomous and at least provisionally isolated individual. But in neither case is any final or ultimate significance ascribed to the concrete historical traditions in which men and women participate.

In the tradition of theological existentialism which Kierkegaard and Bultmann represent, this abstraction of true existence from ordinary historical development in space and time is especially pronounced: the religious or faithful life requires total obedience to the eternal—an inner authenticity that is in principle independent of the external historical life of one's society and culture. But this tendency to abstract authentic existence from ordinary historical life is not confined to religious or theological existentialism. Heidegger's *Being and Time* may serve to epitomize the same tendency in ostensibly secular existentialism. Heidegger does, to be sure, write extensively about the historicity of human being. This historicity is, however, irreducibly individual. Persons create or project their own futures. The result is that both the future and the past are real only in relation to the individual. Heidegger acknowledges that in addition to this individual historicity, there is a world-time or a time that continues after the individual dies. But that time is irrelevant to the individual's achievement of authenticity.

Confirmation of this irreducibly individualistic focus is provided in Heidegger's analysis of social relations. Heidegger states that "being-with" (*Mitsein*) is one of the fundamental structures of human being in the world. Yet his most extensive discussion of being-with—the fourth chapter of the first division in *Being and Time*—focuses on the inauthentic forms of being-with as they are evidenced in the everyday conformist existence of the "they" (*das Man*). This emphasis is, moreover, maintained throughout the book and is supported in Heidegger's analysis of related issues. The discussions of death and of conscience, for example, are insistent in their contention that the authentic individual is the one who stands resolutely alone and responds without dependence on others. Hence the words "independent" (*selbstständig*) and "dependent" (*unselbstständig*) are correlated with authentic and inauthentic existence, respectively. Indeed, the very word translated as "authentic" bears connotations of individuality, since the German *eigentlich* is an elaborated adjectival form of the stem *eigen,* which has the root meaning of "own" or "individual" or "proper." It is accordingly not surprising that Heidegger's use of the word translated somewhat limply as "mineness" offers negative confirmation of his discussions of being-with. The German *Jemeinigkeit* is Heidegger's own creation and has along with "mineness" the meaning of "for ever" or "in every case"—with the result that it suggests an ever present or unavoidable individuality. As in the case of being-with, mineness is said to characterize every human being whatsoever. But whereas being-with figures prominently in discussions of the inauthentic mode of being, mineness is consistently correlated with authenticity.

Detailed documentation of the tendency toward individualism at the expense of positive attention to social and cultural traditions would, of course, require a study in its own right in the case of *Being and Time* alone, not to mention other existentialist works. This documentation could be provided—were the issue sufficiently controversial to warrant it. That is not, however, the case. In their reaction against the social and cultural traditions of their times, the thinkers who most profoundly shaped existentialism as a movement self-consciously described the authentic individual as standing over against conventional historical life. There have, to be sure, been differing judgments about that stance in the interim. As late as 1955, a series of lectures like Bultmann's *History and Eschatology* still advanced a systematic position which carefully abstracts the authenticity of the individual's living from more inclusive historical developments. In contrast, the movement of the later Sartre toward Marxism indicates an attempt to socialize the radical individualism of earlier forms of existentialism. But despite some differences in emphasis, the existentialist movement in its most influential expressions did and typically still does tend to an individualism which either disparages or ignores historical traditions and as a result does not focus on the question of mediation over space and time more comprehensive than a single life span.

Mediation and the Alternative to Existentialism and Zen

The question of mediation may serve to epitomize the differences between Zen and existentialism on the one hand and what I have termed the third or Hegel type on the other. For in contrast to both Zen and existentialism, this third type takes historical process to be ultimately significant. Differentiation in space and development over time are not construed to be in the last analysis illusory, as they are in Zen. Nor is world history viewed as irrelevant to the attainment of an authentic humanity, as it is in existentialism. Instead, historical processes are interpreted as intimately related not only to the possibility of faithful living for the individual but also to the realization of the ends toward which the cosmos itself is affirmed to be moving.

The emphasis on the significance of mediation which distinguishes this third type from the existentialist and Zen positions is significantly parallel to the differences between Peirce's Thirdness and his Firstness and Secondness. In discussing Thirdness with reference to cultural representation and social norms and conventions, Peirce calls attention to the inherence of symbolic processing or mediation in every dimension of human life. Language itself is the most pervasive example of the dependence of experience on the traditions through which it is perceived and articulated. And such examples as those of giving and contract-making are more specific illustrations of the extent to which more or less elaborate conventions inform much of human interaction. Peirce does insist that Firstness and Secondness are as fundamental to human experience as is Thirdness. But in contrast to positions which focus on immediate experience alone, he maintains that any adequate worldview must include serious and positive attention to the dynamics of social and cultural processes as well.

The emphasis of this third position on historical process—the very emphasis which most sharply distinguishes it from both Zen and existentialism—is at the same time a crucial resource for combining the strengths of the other two perspectives. Like Zen, the third position is holistic: it affirms all of reality for what it can become. And like existentialism, the third position is critical: it continually calls into question claims to final adequacy in the present state of affairs through reference to the ultimate or ideal order which is affirmed as its destiny. In short, in historicizing the Zen type, the third position systematically integrates the critical stance of existentialism into a perspective which nonetheless appreciates and even ultimately affirms the whole of reality.

Perhaps the most imposing instance of this third type is the philosophy of Hegel. In any case, Hegel's thought is an appropriate focus for exploring the third type if for no reason other than his enormous influence. Both in its own right and through its impact on the thought of others like Marx, the philosophy of Hegel has profoundly affected the social and cultural history of the world. But its influence is not in fact all that commends it for detailed consideration as an illustration of the third type. There are at least two other reasons. The first is that Hegel himself conceived of his philosophy as an alternative to positions analogous to the existentialist and Zen types as I have outlined them. And the second is that Hegel's thought in my judgment constitutes an achievement in philosophy yet to be surpassed in its systematic power and scope.

The Philosophy of Hegel: An Advance Beyond the Existentialist Type

To speak of Hegel's thought as an advance beyond existentialism is at the very least anachronistic. For those who sympathize with the existentialist reaction against Hegel's system, it must in addition appear as provocative and even as unfair. But Hegel does self-consciously formulate his position as an immanent critique of and advance beyond a perspective systematically analogous to the existentialist type. That perspective is the thought of the Enlightenment in general and, more frequently than not, of Kant in particular.

Hegel emphatically views his critique as an advance from within. Although all of Hegel's works deal with his relationship to the Enlightenment in one form or another, he expresses his position most dramatically in the section in the *Phenomenology of Mind* on the Enlightenment, with its extended comparison between "belief" and "pure insight." The structure of the entire section may serve to epitomize his line of argument; for the conflict between "belief" and "insight" becomes a conflict within the Enlightenment perspective itself. During the Enlightenment, even orthodoxy as Hegel describes it is in the end unable to repudiate the virtually exclusive focus on this world that characterizes the age. What Hegel terms "belief" accordingly elaborates a Deism precisely parallel to the most consistent materialism of the day. This Deism is like the materialism it claims to reject in that it confines its attention utterly to the finite while at the same time affirming an unknowable beyond. Deism affirms this unknowable beyond as God. It is, however, in Hegel's view analogous to the abstraction of pure matter which the materialists posit. In both cases, what is posited or affirmed serves only to redirect attention to the finite world. Hegel maintains that this development is necessary. Only through this preoccupation with the finite could the self-confidence of the individual assert itself over against previously unquestioned authorities. Accordingly, any advance beyond the position of true insight must build on "the truth of Enlightenment" that "both worlds are reconciled and heaven is transplanted to earth below."[13]

The most vivid expression of Hegel's critique of the Enlightenment position is his appropriation of traditional theological language about the crucifixion of Christ. For example, in the highly rhetorical passage concluding his 1802 work *Faith and Knowledge,* he refers to "the speculative Good Friday" which demonstrates that the Enlightenment's absolutizing of the finite—a development which Hegel sees captured in the outcry "God is dead"—is a crucial moment, "but also not more than a moment," in the life of spirit.[14] More characteristically, Hegel correlates this "speculative" or philosophical statement with a description of what he takes to be the effect of the crucifixion of Christ on the consciousness of the believer. An extended passage in the *Phenomenology of Mind* illustrates his procedure:

When the death of the mediator is grasped by the self, this means the sublation [both transcendence and preservation] of his factuality, of his particular independent existence. . . . On the other side . . . the death of the mediator is not merely death of his *natural* aspect, of his particular self-existence: what dies is . . . also the abstraction of the divine being. . . . That death is the bitterness of feeling of the "unhappy consciousness," when it feels that God Himself is dead. . . . This feeling . . . means, in point of fact, the loss of the substance and of its objective existence over against consciousness.[15]

Because this passage illustrates (and in turn presupposes) a number of Hegel's technical terms, it is not readily intelligible in all its details apart from an understanding of the system as a whole. But the thrust of Hegel's line of argument may be summarized without explication of all his technical terminology. The crucifixion of Christ epitomizes two converse but complementary movements which are both required if the perspective of the Enlightenment is to be transcended. On the one hand, the individual self must come to see that it is not a discrete and isolated entity which in itself is of absolute validity. And on the other hand, the abstraction of a divine being or substance standing over against humankind must be allowed to die. The result of this double movement is that Hegel is able to affirm the human dignity and moral self-consciousness which the Enlightenment glorified while at the same time conceiving of persons as ingredient in and finally subordinate to that comprehending life of spirit of which they are moments.

In this commentary on the Enlightenment, Hegel in effect at the same time criticizes the preoccupation of the existentialist type with the individual self confronting an alien environment over against it. His response is to reconceive both the self and the environment so that the two are seen to be in intimate, unavoidable, and at least potentially positive correlation. This position is not infrequently formulated with reference to traditional theological categories. It is not, however, restricted to this vocabulary. The same systematic criticism and response is, for example, expressed politically. It then takes the form of a rejection of every individualism which fails to stress the self's incorporation into more comprehensive wholes to which are owed some measure of not uncritical allegiance. Similarly, Hegel's position is expressed in such philosophical discussions as those on what he terms the true and the spurious infinite. The issue in this case is no doubt one common to the theological and the philosophical traditions. It is, however, less dependent on explicitly religious imagery than is his consideration of Christ's death.

The object of Hegel's criticism in his discussions of the true and spurious infinite is again the Enlightenment position in its various forms. Whether this position is formulated theologically, as it is for eighteenth-century Deism, or ethically, as it is for Kant and Fichte, it entails a "finitized infinite"—an ascription of infinity to what is itself finite. For Deism that spurious infinite is a deity defined as beyond the world; and for Kant and Fichte, it is the object of a "perennial ought" which is conceived as always beyond what the human agent in fact attains. Hegel summarizes the contradiction concisely:

This contradiction occurs as a direct result of the circumstance that the finite remains . . . opposed to the infinite so that there are two determinatenesses. . . . The infinite is only the limit of the finite and is thus only a determinate infinite, *an infinite which is itself finite.*[16]

As his own positive contrast to this spurious infinite, Hegel elaborates a conception of the true infinite which reiterates his rejection of any final opposition between the finite and its ultimate environment:

Infinity *is* only as a transcending of the finite; it therefore essentially contains its other and is, consequently, in its own self the other of itself. The finite is not sublated by a power existing outside it; on the contrary, its infinity consists in sublating its own self.[17]

The finite cannot, in short, stand over against the true infinite—a contention which follows from the very definition of infinity as not limited. As Hegel observes, "One only needs to *be aware of what one is saying* in order to find the determination of the finite in the infinite."[18] The result is, of course, that Hegel rejects the unqualified individualism not only of the Enlightenment position as he portrays it but also of the existentialist type and instead propounds a holistic metaphysic no less comprehensive than that of Zen.

The Philosophy of Hegel: An Historicizing of the Zen Type

Though Hegel maintains that the finite is ingredient in the infinite, he does not simply deny the opposition between the finite and the infinite. He insists instead that the true infinite must be conceived as a process, a becoming, through which the opposition between the finite and the (spurious) infinite is continuously overcome. Hegel very deliberately contrasts his position to every glorification of an undifferentiated unity between the finite and the infinite. The exemplars of this perspective to which he refers most frequently are the Eleatics, Spinoza, and the Hindu philosophy with which he was familiar. These and all other representatives of what I have outlined as the Zen type he dismisses with an epigram. They, like Schelling, affirm an absolute which may be characterized as "the night in which all cows are black."[19] To espouse this position after the Enlightenment in Hegel's view constitutes an undialectical repudiation of the radical individualism and self-consciousness which the eighteenth century represents. In opposition to this rejection of all differentiation, Hegel affirms "the finite as it is in the true infinite—as a determination, a content, which is distinct but is not an *independent, self-subsistent* being, but only a *moment*."[20]

Hegel epitomizes the difference between his own position and that of an undifferentiated monism in contrasting the conceptions of substance and subject:

In my view—a view which the developed exposition of the system itself can alone justify—everything depends on grasping and expressing the ultimate truth not as Substance but as Subject as well.[21]

"Substance" is associated with the monism of Spinoza, which conceives of the absolute as a static entity comprehensible through a deductive methodology modeled on the procedure of geometry. In contrast, "Subject" suggests movement or development—with reference both to human subjectivity and to the grammatical subject of a sentence, which in requiring the further specification involved in its predicate unavoidably entails mediation to be complete. Hegel intends this double reference. For not only human knowing but also the ultimate object of knowledge are in the process of development. Hegel summarizes the correlation:

The truth is the whole. The whole, however, is merely the essential nature reaching its completeness through the process of its own development. Of the Absolute it must be said that it is essentially a result, that only at the end is it what it is in very truth; and just in that consists its nature, which is to be actual, subject, or self-becoming, self-development.[22]

That the absolute or the whole or the infinite or God is said to be in the process of its own development is the ultimate indication of Hegel's concern with mediation over time. This development is, moreover, intimately related to the concrete data of history. Indeed, the central means through which the absolute attains its ends is human activity:

A principle, a law[,] is something implicit, which as such, however true in itself, is not completely real (actual). . . . That which is in itself is a possibility, a faculty. It has not yet emerged out of its implicitness into existence. A second element must be added for it to become reality, namely, activity, actualization. The principle of this is the will, man's activity in general. It is only through this activity that the concept and its implicit ("being-in-themselves") determinations can be realized, actualized; for of themselves they have no immediate efficacy. The activity which puts them in operation and in existence is the need, the instinct, the inclination, and passion of man.[23]

The actions of finite spirit are, in short, constitutive of the activity of infinite or absolute spirit.

In Hegel's portrayal, this awareness of the absolute as inclusive of and intimately related to finite persons first emerges into human self-consciousness in the religious cult and pre-eminently in the Christian mass. But he emphasizes repeatedly and forcefully that this religiously imaged reconciliation must in turn be fully actualized in every sphere of life. In Hegel's vocabulary, that means the state—the word which he uses to include all of human social and cultural existence. The goal of this development is, then, willing participation of independently valuable persons in a comprehensive spiritual order in which the ends of the community are in the last analysis one with those of the individuals who constitute it.

If only because his interpreters have not always agreed on the point, it may be necessary to underscore the fact that Hegel does view historical development as ultimately significant. There are, unfortunately, occasional passages in which his meaning is less than unambiguous. The most notorious instance is a passage in which Hegel appears to maintain that the good is fully accomplished and hence that it is necessary only to remove the illusion of its not being already actualized. This passage occurs in an editorial addition to paragraph 212 of the *Encyclopedia*—an addition which was published for the first time in the 1840 version prepared under the auspices of an association of Hegel's friends and former students. Accordingly, the text itself has very little authority—and can scarcely justify interpreting Hegel as the exponent of an abstract and undifferentiated monism indistinguishable from what he consistently rejects in Schelling or Spinoza. Yet that is precisely the direction in which Hegel is pressed in such works as F. H. Bradley's *Appearance and Reality* (1893), J. E. McTaggart's *Studies in Hegelian Cosmology* (1902), and P. T. Raju's *Thought and Reality: Hegelianism and Advaita* (1937).

What Hegel does argue is that, in the historical process as in any teleological activity, the ideal in fact realizes only itself:

It can therefore be said of the teleological activity that in it the end is the beginning, the consequent the ground, that it is a becoming of what has become, that in it only what already exists comes into existence.[24]

In so conceiving teleological activity, Hegel is concerned with countering the Kantian tendency to mortgage the present to the future. In contrast to this tendency, Hegel insists that men and women participate in the present in the actualization of the ends of spirit: the ultimate order is not lost in an indefinite future but is rather the very ground or presupposition of the present and as such is in the process of self-realization.

The philosophical formulation of ultimate truth may abstract from particular temporal reference, as Hegel's heuristic ideal of "absolute knowledge" does. But because the content of that truth is the systematic conception of the end toward which the whole of reality is in process, it presupposes and therefore includes within itself the entire course of its historical development. Similarly, the political philosopher may equate the actual and the rational, as Hegel does in the preface to the *Philosophy of Right*. But that equation assumes Hegel's definition of actuality as that which expresses the ultimate teleological order—a designation not automatically accorded to every state of affairs.[25] Despite occasional ambiguities, Hegel does not, then, simply affirm all that is or, in political terms, uncritically legitimate the *status quo*. Hegel does not, in short, illustrate the Zen type. Instead he is systematically committed to the significance of historical development. For only through that development does the ultimate community which is absolute spirit realize itself.

The Third Type and Adequacy to Experience

The argument for the greater adequacy of the third type in comparison with the positions of existentialism and Zen is already implicit in the order of the foregoing exposition and in the issues on which that exposition focuses. It is, moreover, explicit in my contention that this third type has resources for combining the strengths of the other two positions that are unavailable on other premises. But it may still be helpful to reiterate and amplify the case for this claim to greater adequacy.

As I have attempted to show, both in the preceding chapter and by correlating the types with Peirce's categories of Firstness and Secondness in this chapter, Zen and existentialism take a very particular dimension or form of experience as illuminating all of reality. In the case of Zen, this experience is one of at-homeness or belonging inclusion in an encompassing and in some sense benevolent whole. For existentialism, the normative experience is that of opposition, of standing over against, of sensing a claim or demand on the self. Both of these forms of experience are recurrent patterns in the history of religions. They are the experience of the mystic and the prophet, of union with the divine and confrontation with the holy and wholly other. But no matter how crucial such particular religious forms or dimensions of experience may be in their own right, they may be generalized as the clue to all experience only with the greatest of care. Indeed, if the effect of generalizing from either the mystical or the prophetic experience is not to be the isolation of religion from all other forms of life, the emphasis on direct or immediate union or encounter must be qualified so that there is some point of contact with the temporally and spatially mediated existence of human communities.

The difficulties that derive from generalizing the particular experiences which inform positions like those of existentialism and Zen are especially pronounced in the "modern" religious situation. The reason is that the simplest line of implication from taking unmediated union or encounter as normative leads to the dualism of "historic religion." In this case, the other order of reality revealed in the religious dimension of experience is strictly and programmatically unintelligible in human terms. Conversely, the sense of the real derivative from union or encounter with the divine or the ultimate is not directly applicable to everyday life. Zen and existentialism do not, however, appeal to this kind of metaphysical dualism. Consequently they are in the position of affirming radical epistemological or ethical discontinuity after rejecting the dualistic ontology which most readily renders such discontinuity conceivable.

The third or Hegel type concurs with the thrust toward ethical and epistemological transcendence evidenced in the existentialist and the Zen positions. It recognizes, in short, that the world as it is requires both new vision and creative action in order to become transformed into that all-inclusive community which is affirmed as its destiny. The third type does not, however, contend that this critical stance presupposes dynamics discontinuous with those informing all of historical existence. Accordingly, it does not interpret the experience of the mystic or the prophet as direct or unmediated in contrast to all other dynamics of personal, social, and cultural life. Instead, it recognizes the distinctive character and value of such forms of experience without isolating them or obscuring the extent to which they presuppose, are mediated through, and in turn influence concrete historical traditions.

Because the third type is generalized from the individual's participation in social life, it can account for ranges of experience that the existentialist and Zen types either ignore or denigrate. I have in mind here such formative processes as the learning of language, the development of affective and cognitive skills, and the appropriation of central values and social roles. That the third type can take seriously the dynamics informing personal, social, and cultural life is the source of its power in illuminating contemporary experience. It is, as I have argued, especially striking that positive attention to historical life allows the third type to integrate into its conceptuality the central commitments of the other two positions. This capacity of the third type to affirm the truth of both existentialism and Zen is especially relevant to any religious worldview, for it is religiously crucial to affirm both that human actions toward creating community are significant and that the very structure of the real itself supports this action. In contrast, to assert the significance of human action as independent of its ontological grounding is to subscribe to an idolatry of the human individual—as the existentialist type does. And to affirm all that is without insisting on the need for transforming action is to lend uncritical legitimation to the *status quo*—as the Zen type does.

The Third Type in Recent Eastern Religious Thought

The alternative to existentialism and Zen as I have outlined it is like the other two positions in that it too may be construed as a type. Like the existentialist and the Zen positions, this third alternative may be expressed through the symbolic resources of different traditions. Perhaps the most influential worldwide example of the type is Marxism in its various forms. The same commitment to the significance of historical development is, however, also evident in the western religious traditions which Marxism self-consciously attempts to secularize. The concern of prophetic Judaism with historical life is no doubt relevant to Marx's own development and is in any case an imposing instance of this perspective. Similarly, the entire Augustinian-Calvinist perspective in Christian theology also tends toward this pattern—even if it does, in its traditional formulations, insist on a final discontinuity between history and its eschatological consummation. The centrality of this tendency in traditional theology may be epitomized in the figures of Augustine and Calvin themselves, and of a Calvinist like Jonathan Edwards. There are, moreover, heirs to this perspective who so emphasize the continuity between historical processes and their ultimate fulfillment that they conceive the former as developing directly into the latter. Among twentieth-century thinkers, Walter Rauschenbusch, advocate of the American social gospel, and post-World War II German theologian Wolfhart Pannenberg illustrate this position. And, although he can scarcely be considered an heir of Calvin, Roman Catholic Pierre Teilhard de Chardin approaches the same systematic conclusions as do Rauschenbusch and Pannenberg.

This third type also has its proponents in the East. Influential examples include the Hindu philosopher Sri Aurobindo and the Japanese Buddhist thinker Susumu Yamaguchi. That thinkers who identify with Hindu and Buddhist traditions may be interpreted as illustrating this type is especially significant in view of the tendency in both the East and the West to equate Oriental wisdom with one variant or another of the Zen type. Thinkers like Aurobindo and Yamaguchi are not, to be sure, typical interpreters of their respective traditions. But they do nonetheless represent the increasing importance of the third type even in cultures which have traditionally emphasized other perspectives. Hence they illustrate the process through which the varying resources of a tradition may receive different emphases or even systematically modified interpretations as its adherents encounter changing ranges of experience.

In the case of Sri Aurobindo, the process of modification is sufficiently pronounced that some traditional Indian philosophers refuse even to acknowledge his thought as Hindu. Yet Aurobindo himself insists on interpreting his experience through the resources of Hindu thought and practice. He is persuaded that every viable religious philosophy must be able to do justice to such critical dimensions of his contemporary experience as the remarkable growth of political self-consciousness in India and the correlative awareness of the innovative capacities of technology and social activism. So he seeks to integrate such dimensions of experience into a Hindu vision of reality.

Because his writings are voluminous, even the most cursory summary of Aurobindo's thought is beyond the scope of this discussion. But his most ambitious work, *The Life Divine,* does nonetheless contain a chapter which may serve to document his adherence to the third type. The chapter is entitled "The Integral Knowledge and the Aim of Life: Four Theories of Existence." In it Aurobindo contrasts his "integralizing view" to three other positions: the supracosmic, the cosmic and terrestrial, and the supraterrestrial or otherworldly.[26] The third is the equivalent of Bellah's "historic religion": this world is viewed as a time of temporary passage to be dedicated to ethical or spiritual discipline with the aim of immortality in another world or plane of existence. In contrast to this dualistic view, the cosmic and the supracosmic positions insist that there is only one reality. The former sees the natural universe as exhausting the real; the latter posits a supreme reality and conceives of this world as an illusion or at least as having no enduring significance.

Aurobindo is concerned about the conceptualizing of the cosmic and the supracosmic as mutually exclusive alternatives. In particular, he wants to counter the "world-abolishing" impulse of the supracosmic position. Aurobindo attributes this position to "the Buddhists" and acknowledges that Vedāntic thought tends in the same direction. But he insists that the Vedāntic tradition also has resources for the affirmation of the world precisely in its development:

In the Vedanta of the Upanishads, the Becoming of Brahman is accepted as a reality; there is room therefore for the truth of Becoming.[27]

And this processive or evolutionary position is the one to which Aurobindo himself subscribes:

Earth-life is not a lapse into the mire of something undivine, vain, miserable, offered by some Power to itself as a spectacle or to the embodied soul as a thing to be suffered and then cast away from it: it is the scene of the evolutionary unfolding of the being which moves towards the revelation of a supreme spiritual light and power and joy and oneness, but includes in it also the manifold diversity of the self-achieving spirit.[28]

In short, after outlining "theories of existence" parallel to the existentialist and Zen types, Aurobindo articulates and affirms an alternative systematically analogous to the third or Hegel position.

Like Aurobindo, Susumu Yamaguchi represents a commitment among Asian religious thinkers to a holistic and processive perspective. Yamaguchi is a priest in the Otani branch of the Shin sect and the president of and a teacher at Otani University. (It is worth noting that more than half of Japanese Buddhists belong to one or another Pure Land school, of which the Shin sect is by far the largest.) Yamaguchi is emphatic in rejecting not only all dualistic positions but also the supracosmic perspective to which Aurobindo incorrectly assigns all Buddhists. Instead of annulling or abolishing the world in a supracosmic reality, Buddhism, as Yamaguchi interprets it, is dedicated to the purification and transformation of precisely that world. He summarizes this affirmation concisely with reference to the image of the Pure Land that is central to his tradition:

Pure Land is the most excellent fruit of the practice of the Middle Way, it is the world constituted by the action of the great compassion.[29]

Echoing a frequent Mahāyāna criticism of the Theravāda concern with withdrawal in the interest of individual realization and example, Yamaguchi's interpretation of Buddhism entails a rejection of the religious strategy of retreat from the world:

In order to discover the infinite existence, we have to abandon the unreal supermundane life and go out into the real world, because it lies beyond the reach of the monks and hermits who have forsaken the world. In the real world, however, we should not attach to ourselves and our possessions as might be expected there, but destroy and annihilate attachment to ourselves and our possessions.[30]

Yamaguchi is not, however, criticizing only Theravāda Buddhism. He is also concerned to distinguish his position from that of every nonhistorical orientation. This concern is perhaps most evident in his programmatic rejection of direct or unmediated deliverance in favor of an emphasis on the necessity for mediation through a concrete historical tradition:

The Buddhist is not expected to accept a mystic view advocating the mystic union which would directly unite us to the Buddha without mediation of Sākyamuni's preaching which consists of worldly thoughts and words.[31]

In other passages, he is even more emphatic in insisting on the necessity of this historical mediation. He maintains, for example, that "we should not have been able to share the benefit of the great vow of the great compassion, if we had no other recourse but to appeal direct to the Lord Amita" and that "a miracle of the ordinary man in this world being direct[ly] favoured with Amita's Light would be impermissible in Buddhism."[32]

This rejection of direct and unmediated union with the ultimate constitutes a systematic contrast between Yamaguchi's thought and the Zen type. Zen Buddhism does, to be sure, also affirm the importance of a succession of patriarchs. But in contrast to Zen's emphasis on the self's attainment of undifferentiated union with the real, Yamaguchi insists on the validity, on the truth, on the reality of differentiated existence. This insistence is what is at stake in Yamaguchi's double affirmation of the preaching as well as the meditating Buddha —of the dynamic as well as the static Buddha, to use the terminology of his title.

Yamaguchi espouses the primacy of the meditative Buddha:

The preaching and active Buddha and the meditative and tranquil Buddha are the same in essence, and the latter is the primary aspect.[33]

Yet he also insists that this meditation is in the service of, indeed integral to, historical action:

He would not be the meditative Buddha if he didn't emancipate the beings by means of preaching when he is absorbed in the meditation of
emptiness. . . . The raison d'être of the meditative Buddha consists in
that his preaching is available for people because of his absorption in the
meditation of emptiness. . . . Missing of this point will produce a misunderstanding that Buddhism is a religion of the hermits who renounce
the world and seek to be absorbed in the supermundane meditation of
emptiness. This will lead people to believe that Buddhism is good-for-
nothing in the actual world.[34]

The concern evident in this extended quotation to emphasize the
this-worldly relevance of Buddhism is also illustrated in Yamaguchi's
interpretations of such central Mahāyāna conceptions as the emptiness or suchness of all existence. He expresses the tradition's criticism
of all views of reality as consisting of discrete substances. In contrast
to every such view, Yamaguchi insists on the Buddhist position of
interdependent origination. In elaborating this position in a chapter
subtitled "The Pure Threefold Circle," Yamaguchi discusses the example of giving. His analysis is very similar to that of Peirce as he
argues that only the threefold structure of giver, gift, and receiver can
do justice to the situation—as opposed to every interpretation which
focuses on the dyadic relation of giver and receiver apart from the
total gestalt or structure of donation. Using traditional Buddhist categories, Yamaguchi terms this complexly mediated analysis of existence "the imaginary structure" or "the nominal formation." He recognizes the danger that this designation is "liable to lead to the
conception of life which is expressed as 'the life is an evanescent so-
journ,' " but he argues that the intention of the tradition is only to
criticize theories "that admit the existence of the things in general
which are not conceived as originated interdependently." Accordingly, he concludes that awareness of the complex interdependence of
the processes constituting existence is not imaginary in the sense of
illusory but rather a complex interpretation of the meaning of emptiness:

Therefore the imaginary structure denotes the valid mode of human existence from the point of view of interdependent origination.[35]

Historical existence is not, then, an illusion perpetuated by social life
in general and language in particular; rather it is in itself crucial to
that reality of the Pure Land which Yamaguchi celebrates.

Christian Theology and the Third Type

In discussing the alternative to existentialism and Zen in recent religious thought, I have focused on the writings of Aurobindo and Yamaguchi and referred only cursorily to western traditions because I want to conclude this study with a consideration of resources in Christian theology for expressing the commitments systematized in the third type.

Those resources are very impressive. The biblical account of creation together with its elaboration in the theological tradition already testifies to the fundamental concern of Christian symbolism with the cosmos and its providential ordering. Still more relevant are the theological preoccupations with redemption, sanctification, and eschatological consummation—preoccupations which involve interest not exclusively in heavenly fulfillment for the faithful but rather also in personal and social transformation within history. The incipient biblical and fully developed patristic dogma of the incarnation along with the doctrine of the church as in some sense the continuation of the incarnation may serve to epitomize this emphasis on transformation in history. For what is distinctive about the dogma of the incarnation is its insistence—against the dominant tendency of Greek philosophy, for example—that God is intimately involved with both the travail and the destiny of the world.

To observe that the Christian tradition includes substantial resources for affirming both a benevolent cosmic order and the significance of historical development is not to assert that this tradition as a whole illustrates the third type. It does not. Indeed, the prevailing perspective in traditional Christianity does not exemplify any of the alternatives which I have outlined as responses to the "modern" religious situation. Instead, the dominant tendency of Christian theological reflection and even more of conventional Christian piety conforms to the pattern of Bellah's "historic religion." Accordingly, every approach which qualifies the metaphysical dualism of this position entails a systematic reformulation of the prevailing worldview of New Testament documents and of much of the history of Christian thought and piety. Insofar as the line of argument I have advanced in this study is persuasive, some such systematic reformulation is, however, unavoidable. Of the tasks which this line of argument assigns to theology, the one remaining is, therefore, to appropriate the symbolism of the tradition so as to express that position which most adequately interprets and in turn shapes contemporary experience. The next and final chapter addresses this question of Christian commitment beyond existentialism and Zen.

Notes

1. *Collected Papers of Charles Sanders Peirce,* A. W. Burks, C. Hartshorne, and P. Weiss, eds. (Cambridge: Harvard University Press, 1931-58), vol. 8, para. 329. The letter to Lady Welby, from which this phrase is quoted, provides a concise summary of Peirce's categorial scheme. See vol. 8, pp. 220-31. For a more detailed exposition of the categorial scheme, see vol. 1, pp. 141-80.
2. Ibid. vol. 1, para. 343.
3. Ibid. vol. 1, para. 303.
4. Ibid. vol. 1, para. 303.
5. Ibid. vol. 1, para. 328.
6. Ibid., vol. 8, para. 324.
7. Ibid. vol. 1, para. 324.
8. Ibid. vol. 8, para. 330.
9. Ibid. vol. 1, para. 345.
10. Ibid. vol. 1, para. 475.
11. Ibid. vol. 1, para. 480.
12. Ibid. vol. 8, para. 331.
13. G. W. F. Hegel, *The Phenomenology of Mind,* J. B. Baillie, tr. (New York: Harper & Row–Torchbooks, 1967), pp. 597-98.
14. G. W. F. Hegel, *Erste Druckschriften,* G. Lasson, ed. (Leipzig: Verlag von Felix Meiner, 1928), pp. 345-46.
15. Hegel, *The Phenomenology of Mind,* pp. 781-82.
16. *Hegel's Science of Logic,* A. V. Miller, tr. (London: George Allen & Unwin, 1969), pp. 139-40.
17. Ibid. pp. 145-46. The "transcending," "sublated," and "sublating" in the translation are all renderings of the German noun *Aufhebung* and the corresponding past participle *aufgehoben.* Because there is no adequate English equivalent for this crucial Hegelian conception, it is important to remember its dual meanings of "preservation" and "overcoming." Though "sublating" is awkward, it at least has the merit of not emphasizing overcoming to the exclusion of preservation—as "transcendence" tends to do.
18. Ibid. p. 143.
19. Hegel, *Phenomenology of Mind,* p. 79.
20. Hegel, *Science of Logic,* pp. 149-50.
21. Hegel, *Phenomenology of Mind,* p. 80.
22. Ibid. pp. 81-82.
23. G. W. F. Hegel, *Reason in History,* R. S. Hartman, tr. (Cleveland: Bobbs-Merrill, Library of Liberal Arts, 1953), pp. 27-28. The parallel passage in

the older and even less elegant but complete translation of G. W. F. Hegel, *Philosophy of History*, J. Sibree, tr. (New York: Dover Publications, 1956), is on p. 22. With any quotation from the *Philosophy of History* lectures, it is important to note whether the passage in question is from Hegel's own manuscript or a reconstruction from student notes. This particular passage is from Hegel's own manuscript, as indicated in Georg Lasson's critical edition, *Vorlesungen über die Philosophie der Weltgeschichte* (Leipzig: Verlag von Felix Meiner, 1917-20), vol. 1, p. 59.

24. Hegel, *Science of Logic*, p. 748.

25. For a more detailed discussion of Hegel's position with respect both to political analysis and to the philosophical transcendence of time, see my *Christologies and Cultures: Toward A Typology of Religious Worldviews* (Atlantic Highlands, N.J.: Humanities Press, 1974), pp. 129-39.

26. Sri Aurobindo [Ghose], *The Life Divine* (New York: India Library Society, 1965), esp. pp. 594-601.

27. Ibid. p. 596.

28. Ibid. p. 606.

29. Susumu Yamaguchi, *Dynamic Buddha and Static Buddha*, S. Watanabe, tr. (Tokyo: Risosha, 1958), pp. 71-72. For a more general statement of his position, see Yamaguchi's article, "Development of Mahayana Buddhist Beliefs," *The Path of the Buddha*, K. W. Morgan, ed. (New York: Ronald Press, 1956), pp. 153-81, esp. 171-76.

30. Yamaguchi, *Dynamic Buddha and Static Buddha*, p. 68.

31. Ibid. p. 83.

32. Ibid. pp. 78-79, 82.

33. Ibid., pp. 23-24.

34. Ibid. p. 52.

35. Ibid. p. 42, for all the quotations in this paragraph except for the reference to "nominal formation," which Yamaguchi uses on p. 71 as an alternate expression for "imaginary structure." That "imaginary structure" or "nominal formation" is not a pejorative term is especially clear in that discussion on p. 71, since Yamaguchi asserts that "the nominal formation may be called also the excellent reality" and that "the Pure Land is the purest form of the nominal formation." For the analysis of giving to which I refer, see pp. 44-50.

IV

Christian Commitment
Beyond Existentialism and Zen

In the original title of his *Proslogium* the eleventh-century theologian Anselm of Canterbury expressed what remains a classic definition of theology: faith seeking understanding. The theologian responds to the moral and intellectual and aesthetic challenges of the day as a person already decisively formed through the images and actions of a particular tradition. From within the context of commitment to that tradition, the theologian seeks to interpret both the symbolism of faith and the dynamics of contemporary life so as to engage the truth to which the Christian community testifies with experience in the present. Christian theology is thus doubly time-bounded: there is ongoing development both in the theological tradition itself and in the varying contexts in which that tradition is articulated.

The Varying Contexts of Christian Commitment

The interaction of Christian thought and trends in American culture in recent years provides a striking confirmation of this time-boundedness of theological reflection. During the 1960's there was, especially among intellectuals both within and outside of the churches, a widespread and vocal commitment first to social justice for minorities and then to the termination of American involvement in the Vietnam war. The speeches and writings of numerous theologians expressed this succession of commitments. So did the direct or indirect statements of

leaders from artistic and academic communities, liberal political figures, and influential segments of the media. A similar correlation between theological reflection and cultural mood is evident in the 1970's
—although the mood is quite different. The issue which may serve to
epitomize the change is that of environmental crisis: just as the limits
to growth seem to dictate at least a moratorium on aggressive inter-
vention in the natural order, so a yearning for stability and an end to
social activism is a pervasive mood that characterizes theological
reflection as well as other forms of cultural expression.

This characterization of two decades is, of course, a drastic simplification. Insofar as the ethos of the 1960's as I describe it fits the
leadership of the churches better than the membership as a whole, the
contrast is also overstated. But there is nonetheless a significant difference between the moods of the two decades—a difference which is
not without its influence on Christian thought during the period.

To note this influence is not to contend that theology is simply a
reflection of culture. There are, to be sure, lamentably numerous instances of uncritical conformity. Perhaps the most ironic recent case
is that of the 1975 Hartford Appeal, a document prepared at the
initiative and under the guidance of sociologist Peter Berger and theologian Richard John Neuhaus. That polemic, while castigating social
activism and secularized Christianity for compromising the integrity
of the faith, itself illustrates a completely uncritical reflection of the
prevailing interest in retrenchment or at least consolidation in the
broader culture. Instances of this sort can, unfortunately, be cited
from every point on the theological spectrum. But Christian thinkers
and actors also influence their subculture or even the prevailing culture as a whole. In short, theology not only reflects but also shapes its
cultural context.

This plurality of possible relations between theology and culture is
what makes a contrast like that between the 1960's and the 1970's in
America significant for religious commitment. For only through
awareness of current cultural trends can theology discern the specific
temptations and opportunities confronting the individual believer, the
Christian community, and the broader society. Such discernment can
no doubt lead to an uncritical embrace of current fads. It is, however,
also indispensable if theology is to speak effectively to its times and
not simply echo either the prevailing cultural mood or an ethos of the
past.

The contrast between the 1960's and the 1970's is an example of differences in context on a massive societal scale. But crucial differences in situation also are evident in the various stages of an individual's development or in a person's geographical location and socioeconomic status. All such differences in context are especially relevant for theology insofar as it seeks to affirm the strengths of both existentialism and Zen. For the power of this position is precisely that it combines complementary emphases which provide resources for responses appropriate to diverse situations.

The Truth of Existentialism: Demands of the Kingdom

The existentialist strain in Christian imagery and action is ineradicable. That it is ineradicable is both a normative claim and a descriptive statement. It is normative in the sense that the demand for unqualified obedience is at the very heart of Jewish and Christian religious experience—as the authoritative centrality of the Exodus traditions and the cross of Christ indicates. But it is also a descriptive statement in the sense that the demand for obedience is again and again expressed even though—or better, precisely because—Christians and Jews perennially seek to avoid this central emphasis in the tradition.

The figures of Abraham and Moses and prophets like Amos and Micah and Jeremiah already etch the existentialist motif in sharp relief. The solitary individual stands over against the prevailing mores or the established order of the time. Abraham is of particular interest with reference to existentialism because of his role as the prototypical person of faith in Kierkegaard's Fear and Trembling. There Abraham appears as the utterly obedient believer who heeds the divine word even when obedience requires violation of the highest human standards and the sacrifice of what is of greatest value—in this case, Isaac, the child of promise. Whether this reading of the Genesis accounts is defensible in view of the already existing Canaanite tradition of child sacrifice is no doubt debatable. But for Christian faith Abraham has nonetheless taken on the qualities that Kierkegaard so skillfully portrays. Similarly, Moses and the prophets illustrate in paradigmatic form the stance of the representative of God over against those who rely on conventional wisdom. Here loyalty to the divine imperative enables an uncompromising criticism not only of exploitation and injustice but finally of every form of human self-aggrandizement and self-satisfaction.

The prophetic denunciation of moral complacency and religious self-congratulation is also exhibited in radical form in Christian traditions about the preaching of Jesus. In the Synoptic Gospels the scribes and Pharisees personify this stridently castigated tendency: they are blind guides and whitewashed tombs—hypocrites whose piety is for appearance alone. Over against all such attempts at self-justification stands the ever more intense demand of God. Matthew 5 is an imposing illustration of this pattern. Jesus is portrayed as identifying his ministry with the law and the prophets:

Think not that I have come to abolish the law and the prophets; I have come not to abolish them but to fulfill them. . . . For I tell you, unless your righteousness exceeds that of the scribes and Pharisees, you will never enter the kingdom of heaven. (Matt. 5.17,20.)

Then follows a series of sayings with variations on the introduction "You have heard that it was said. . . . But I say unto you. . . ." In each case—the prohibitions against murder, adultery, and false oaths; the standards for divorce, retribution, and love of neighbor—the former requirement is so radicalized that only self-deception can result in self-satisfaction. And after the culminating injunction to love not only neighbors but even enemies, the series closes with the assertion "You, therefore, must be perfect, as your heavenly Father is perfect" (Matt. 5.48).

This explicit invoking of the standard of perfection is, to be sure, exceptional in the Gospel traditions. But the demand for radical and total obedience is nonetheless central to the accounts of Jesus' preaching about the kingdom or rule of God. In the imagery of Matthew, the kingdom is like a treasure hidden in a field or a pearl of great value which can be purchased only if all else is sold (Matt. 13.44-46). Or as Luke puts it: "No one who puts his hand to the plow and looks back is fit for the kingdom of God" (Luke 9.62). Even family relationships must be unreservedly subordinated to the divine imperative: only those who do the will of God are acknowledged as Jesus' mother and brothers (Matt. 12.46-50; Mark 3.31-35; Luke 8.19-21); not

even burial of one's father justifies delay in responding to the call of
the kingdom (Matt. 8.22; Luke 9.60). The admittedly still imper-
fect example of the first disciples is the standard to be emulated:
called by Jesus, they immediately stopped what they were doing
(Matt. 4.18-22; Mark 1.16-20) or even, as Luke would have it, left
everything (Luke 5.1-11) and followed him.

It is tempting to dismiss this existentialist strain in Jewish and
Christian traditions as an ethical perfectionism that reveals much
about the character of its adherents and little about sound moral
philosophy or tenable religious conviction. After all, the compulsions
of perfectionists are amply illustrated in all religious traditions—and
certainly not least in those Jewish and Christian communities that
stress uncompromising obedience to the divine commandments. Indeed, it seems possible to locate typical candidates for this ethical perfectionism with respect to such coordinates as age and social status.
The demand for uncompromising obedience to clear ethical impera-
tives finds special resonance with the adolescent and young adult.
And when this demand is combined with a radical critique of existing
practices and even of accepted standards, two interrelated but distinguishable moods are involved: resentment and disillusionment. Ex-
periencing and expressing resentment are outsiders who protest their
exclusion—typically, members of relatively deprived classes or members of racial, sexual, and ethnic groups which are the victims of discrimination. In contrast, disillusionment is the province of those
privileged persons who feel that the powerful of the preceding generation have in their actions betrayed the ideals they profess.

This description of typical candidates for ethical perfectionism
could be carried on in great detail—including appropriate qualifications and references to the theoretical literature and at least a few
empirical studies. Even in this cursory form, the description is, I
think, illuminating at least for protest movements like those of the
1960's. It is, moreover, a corrective to rhetoric which presents ethical
idealism as simply a function of individual volition. But however true
the description may be, it may also nourish the temptation to dismiss
the radical ethical challenge in Christian faith. The description must,
therefore, be entertained only with great circumspection. Otherwise it
serves to encourage indulgence in reductionistic explanations of the
truth of existentialism.

That truth is the conviction to which the prophets testify: there is evil in the world and that evil must be uncompromisingly resisted. The vision to see injustice and deprivation is without question not equally distributed among all age and status groups. That fact only highlights the value of such vision wherever it expresses itself. In particular for the Christian community, it is imperative that the demand for radical obedience be voiced over and over again. Otherwise the churches can continue uninterrupted in their comfortable and all too frequently accustomed position as retreats for the relatively privileged. Every such complacency invites and even demands the iconoclasm of the prophets because it is no less than idolatry: it exalts provincial and more or less self-centered loyalties into the ultimate end of life. This idolatry is that against which the truth of existentialism protests. In Christian symbolism there may be widespread disagreement over how best to speak of that ultimate end of life in positive terms. But there is unanimity in the negative judgment that exaltation of any finite entity into the ultimate is to be condemned as an idolatrous substitution of creature for creator. Despite appearances, this agreement is, moreover, not simply negative. For only through ongoing criticism that relativizes false absolutes can truth emerge. In this sense the truth of existentialism is also the truth as such.

The Truth of Zen: The Good News
of the Gospel

That the truth of existentialism represents only one dimension of Christian faith is already evident in the radicalization of the law in the preaching of Jesus. Because the requirements of the law are intensified beyond the attainable, the self-justification frequently associated with ethical perfectionism is in principle precluded. Indeed, precisely such attempts at self-justification are what the earliest Christian documents are concerned to overcome.

To take the most dramatic instance first, in the Gospels this issue of self-justification structures the stylized contrast between the scribes and Pharisees on the one hand and the publicans and sinners on the other. That the contrast is a highly stylized one should not be overlooked. The publicans, detested tax collectors whose own wealth was dependent on the money they managed to exact over and above what Rome required, become the emblem of the despised sinners who respond to Jesus. And the Pharisees, those devout lay leaders who in the first century were calling for an emphasis on personal piety and on teaching in the synagogue rather than on the priestly mediation central to the temple cult, become the focus for the Gospel portrayal of Jesus' opponents.

Distortions in the image of the Pharisee are especially destructive because virtually all forms of modern Judaism are descendants of this Pharisaic-rabbinic movement. Accordingly, I want explicitly and emphatically to register three observations which in effect indicate the need for great care in using the New Testament accounts: first, that the Jesus of the Gospels himself shares many of the commitments espoused by the Pharisees (including the emphasis on personal piety and rabbinic teaching over against the priestly establishment); second, that the New Testament accounts no doubt owe much to the fact that after the destruction of the temple the Pharisees with their orientation to the synagogue represented the most attractive Jewish alternative to the early church; and third, that this particular polarity between the publican as a type and the Pharisee as a type etches a stark contrast so as to focus a central religious issue and therefore should be used only with great caution as a source for historically accurate reports about those portrayed as the two opposing sides.[1]

Even with all the problems of direct or simple historical identifications, the religious issue in the Gospels is, however, clear. The Pharisees are again and again denounced not because they are more reprehensible than others when measured against the standards of the law, but rather because they so exalt themselves that they cannot acknowledge their need. The parable of the Pharisee and the publican is an unambiguous statement of this theme (Luke 18.9-14). So is the parable of the two sons (Matt. 21.28-32). Even the most vituperative denunciations of the Pharisees—those collected in Matthew 23, for example—are, moreover, directed against dwelling on distinctions which allow self-exaltation over against others and hence prevent the contrite recognition of one's own need. As the writer of the Fourth Gospel puts it in the carefully crafted conclusion to the story about Jesus' healing of the man born blind:

Jesus said, "For judgment I came into this world, that those who do not see may see, and that those who see may become blind." Some of the

Pharisees near him heard this, and they said to him, "Are we also blind?" Jesus said to them, "If you were blind, you would have no guilt; but now that you say, 'We see,' your guilt remains." (John 9.39-41.)

The same concentration on the issue of self-justification is evident in the Johannine and Pauline epistles. Characteristic is a summary of the Christian message in the first letter of John:

If we say we have no sin, we deceive ourselves, and the truth is not in us. If we confess our sins, he is faithful and just, and will forgive our sins and cleanse us from all unrighteousness. (I John 1.8-9.)

Similarly, the letters of Paul reiterate this theme again and again in interpreting the requirements of the law as an enslaving power from which the faithful are freed because in Christ they are justified or accepted as righteous before God (see esp. Romans 1.16-17; 3.21-26).

This persistent concern throughout the New Testament to over-come the self-righteousness attendant on attempts at self-justification is as central as it is because it is the unavoidable negative correlate of the positive Gospel or good news that constitutes the Christian proclamation. To use Paul's juridical language, this good news is that in Christ persons are justified or accepted as righteous before God. In the language of ritual echoed in the passage quoted from First John, there is cleansing and forgiveness. Or in the Gospel metaphors of healing, the good news is that the blind see and the sick are restored to health. The implication of this message is that persons are sick, sinful, enslaved—that the repentance or transformation for which Jesus calls is needed. The truth of existentialism is, in short, not denied. In the Gospel narratives, that truth is, however, expressed only as the counterpoint to the truth of Zen. For the drama of Jesus' ministry turns on how the words and acts that express the good news of healing, forgiveness, and liberation are received. It is this emphasis on unconditional acceptance—on the truth of Zen—which in turn elic-its antagonism and uncompromisingly reciprocated condemnation.

In the drama of the Gospels, the Pharisees are, then, cast as Jesus' opponents because they reject his message of unconditional divine ac-ceptance. Committed to the necessity of high ethical standards and exemplary moral practice, the Pharisees cannot countenance the proclamation of Jesus that the rule or kingdom of God is open to all who receive it in humility and gratitude. This equality of opportunity makes no allowance for differential accomplishments: the respected no less than the demeaned must repent; the demeaned no less than the respected may embrace the rule of God. Rejecting both equations, the Pharisees can only perceive the message of Jesus as a threat and an indictment.

In contrast to the Pharisees, the publicans and sinners of the Gospel accounts receive Jesus and his message with joy. Both in the reports of his teaching and in the portrayal of his ministry, the Gospels stress the note of rejoicing and celebration which characterizes Jesus' identification with the disreputable strata of his society. Jesus calls the tax collector Matthew or Levi to follow him and then joins in a great feast to celebrate his positive response (Matt. 9.9-13; Mark 2.13-17; Luke 5.27-32). Similarly, he asks to eat with Zacchaeus, a wealthy tax collector, and is received joyfully (Luke 19.1-10). The familiar parables of the lost sheep, the lost coin, and the prodigal son also illustrate the theme of rejoicing over finding what was lost or the return of the wayward (Matt. 18.12-14; Luke 15.1-32). At the borders of these scenes of celebration—either as observers of Jesus' actions or as listeners to his parables—stand the Pharisees. They are characteristically described as murmuring or complaining or grumbling about Jesus' association with the unworthy. The contrast to the festive mood on which each vignette focuses is, in short, complete.

The joy of those who respond affirmatively to the ministry of Jesus is the expression of their humility and gratitude. Aware of their need, they are thankful for the healing, the forgiveness, the liberation that Jesus communicates. Because they have no pretensions to righteousness, Jesus' call for repentance, for turning around, is not a threat. Instead it is the promise of inclusion in the community of the faithful from which they had always felt excluded. This sense of inclusion is, moreover, not in the end simply an affirmation of the particular human fellowship which they experience with Jesus and his followers. It is rather a conviction that this community receives its sustenance from the rule of God that Jesus points to in his parables and addresses as Father.

Jesus' own trust in and loyalty to this encompassing rule of God is portrayed throughout the Gospel narratives. The central and most vivid expression of this stance is the movement that structures all of the Gospels, though Mark in particular: the inexorable progression to the cross. Insofar as confidence in the rule of God also entails obedience to that rule, existentialist as well as Zen emphases are involved. Frequently the two motifs are inseparable, as in the Garden of Gethsemane when Jesus commits himself to endure the suffering before him: "Father, if thou art willing, remove this cup from me; nevertheless, not my will, but thine, be done." (Luke 22.42. Compare Matt. 26.39 and Mark 14.36.) But there are also passages in which trust in the benevolence of God's governance or rule becomes virtually the exclusive focus of attention.

No doubt the most eloquent of such passages is the invocation of the lilies and the ravens as examples to be emulated:

Therefore I tell you, do not be anxious about your life, what you shall eat, nor about your body, what you shall put on. For life is more than food, and the body more than clothing. Consider the ravens: they neither sow nor reap, they have neither storehouse nor barn, and yet God feeds them. Of how much more value are you than birds! And which of you by being anxious can add a cubit to his span of life? If then you are not able to do as small a thing as that, why are you anxious about the rest? Consider the lilies, how they grow; they neither toil nor spin; yet I tell you, even Solomon in all his glory was not arrayed like one of these. But if God so clothes the grass which is alive in the field today and tomorrow is thrown into the oven, how much more will he clothe you, O men of little faith? And do not seek what you are to eat and what you are to drink, nor be of anxious mind. For all the nations of the world seek these things; and your Father knows that you need them. Instead seek God's kingdom, and these things shall be yours as well. (Luke 12.22-31. Compare Matt. 6.25-33.)

There is, then, no reason for anxiety. It is in any case of no use; but it is also unnecessary because the rule of God governs benevolently. Humble trust, perceptive appreciation, and joyous gratitude are accordingly the attitudes appropriate to the faithful.

It is of course as possible to dismiss this Zen dimension of Christian faith as it is to ignore its existentialist counterpart. Indeed, it is difficult not to hear, as background noise to the music of a passage like this one, the all too familiar charges of impractical utopianism. As in the case of ethical perfectionism, it also seems possible to specify those for whom this Zen emphasis may have particular resonance.

They are persons whom the social order allows the luxury of being dreamers and aesthetes. Accordingly, the meeting of at least their basic needs is assured—whether it be through accumulated financial resources or access to land on which housing and food is dependably available or guaranteed support from others, as in the case of some artists and researchers, many students, and, at least in the past, many spouses. But no more in the Zen than in the existentialist case should such specification of resonances be allowed to sanction reductionistic explanations. For to lose sight of the truth to which the Zen motif testifies would diminish the capacity of Christian faith to interpret and to nurture this invaluable dimension of human experience.

Christian Faith Between Existentialism and Zen

To take the truths of both existentialism and Zen seriously suggests a rhythm between an unqualified commitment to combating evil and a certain comic distance to one's own efforts founded on a basic trust in the real as such, between intense, active involvement and a relaxed, receptive, letting go, between an acute awareness of temporal directedness and a sense of qualities enduring over time, between a focusing on discrete and definitely located particulars and an attending to general patterns and relationships.

These and parallel polarities may be identified with images of the religious ideal or saint both in the Christian and in other traditions. As I have indicated in the preceding chapter, the virtues or strengths of the two positions are in very general terms analogous to those of the prophet and the mystic, respectively. In terms of more particular Christian theological distinctions, it is, moreover, possible to correlate the polarities with the concerns informing doctrines of justification and sanctification—or with confessional differences between, for example, Lutheran and Calvinist traditions. But before pursuing those parallels in more detail, it may be helpful to specify further how the metaphor of rhythm between polarities illumines the patterns of personal faith, of personal commitment and trust, implied in the attempt to join the strengths of existentialism and Zen.

Not only the illustrative polarities but also the metaphor of rhythm is integral to this formulation. To take the truths of existentialism and

Zen seriously need not mean to aspire to attain both sides of each polarity at every moment. Indeed, it cannot mean that, since the terms may well work against each other with the result that neither the existentialist nor the Zen strength is realized. For example, in the case of unqualified commitment and comic distance, the attempt to espouse both virtues simultaneously can readily lead to a debilitating cynicism. Resolute commitment to an ideal requires an investment of energy and a concentration of attention which can easily be dissipated or distracted if the ambiguities and uncertainties inherent in every enterprise become a simultaneous focus of interest. Yet a certain sense of comic distance is nonetheless a virtue. Only if persons are also aware of the limitations, even the possible absurdities, of the projects to which they are committed can they avoid the dangers of fanaticism and idolatry. The ideal to which the combined truths of existentialism and Zen point is, then, the double capacity to be fully and effectively invested in what one takes to be morally required activity and yet also to be able to stand back and laugh at oneself.

The strengths specified in the polarity between unqualified commitment and comic distance are particularly vulnerable to the attempt to affirm both terms at every moment. With the other illustrative polarities, it is, however, less obvious that both sets of virtues cannot be realized simultaneously. To take an example popularized in Robert Pirsig's recent novel *Zen and the Art of Motorcycle Maintenance,* the intense activity of working on a machine can profitably be combined with a receptivity that respects and therefore can respond to signals from the object or the material at hand. And this merging of activity and receptivity is, of course, even more critical in interaction in social situations. Similarly, it seems possible that the capacity to apprehend particulars and general patterns simultaneously may be developed— though this double apprehensive is more readily imaginable in the case of aesthetic perception of spatial relationships than in the case of contrasting time senses.

Yet despite the possibilities of close correlations between the polar terms, the metaphor of rhythm or movement from one to the other is, I think, apt. The distinction in gestalt psychology between foreground and background may be helpful in imaging or conceiving this movement. The question then becomes whether or not both terms of a given polarity can be in the foreground at the same time. Insofar as the analogy to gestalt psychology is illuminating, the answer is no. Certainly both sets of strengths or virtues may be present. But insofar as, for example, intentional activity is in the foreground, receptivity is in the background. Effective work or successful communication may well require a constant movement between the two terms of the polarity. That rhythm is not, however, the same as simultaneity. Similarly, attention is not in the same moment focused on discrete particulars and general patterns; nor is an acute awareness of temporal directedness compatible with simultaneous abstraction from change over time. Instead, in each case a valuing of both sets of virtues requires a rhythm from one polar term to the other.

In addition to countering the view that both sets of strengths should be simultaneously realized, the metaphor of rhythm may serve to underscore the fact that I am not proposing a kind of compromise between existentialism and Zen. The language of polarities does suggest other possible images—that of mid-point, for example—which do imply precisely this avoiding of two extremes. In contrast to such alternatives, I want to affirm the value of both extremes, of both sets of polar strengths. I emphasize this fact because compromises between such polar terms as intense involvement and letting go result not in the strength of a golden mean but rather in the debilitating weakness of never being either fully engaged or fully disengaged.

The metaphor of rhythm is not a traditional theological rubric. An appreciation for the value of movement back and forth between the polar strengths that the existentialist and the Zen types represent may, however, illumine complementary emphases in Christian reflection on the new life of the faithful. To focus on a particular example within Protestantism, the contrast between the Lutheran and Calvinist traditions on the relative primacy of justification and sanctification involves issues that parallel the various polarities between Zen and existentialism. As anyone who has worked with Lutherans and Calvinists together on specific projects can testify, this contrast is, moreover, not simply a question of abstract theory. Instead it informs the approach of the two communities to even the most concrete of practical issues or problems.

The Lutheran emphasis on justification—on justification by grace through faith—captures in a formula the central theme of the Christian gospel or good news. It is the dominant theme in Jesus' ministry among the outcasts of his time. It is also a governing motif in Paul's theology, programmatically in the first chapters of Romans, but throughout the other letters as well. This theme is simply that there is nothing human beings can do or need to do to make themselves acceptable; for redemption, justification, salvation is already by the grace of God a reality available through faith. The crucial religious issue is, therefore, whether or not persons have faith: whether or not they have a basic trust in God, in the ultimate reality on whom all of life depends. Only such trust allows persons to accept themselves and their fellow human beings. Accordingly, it is only on the basis of this trust that exhortations to commitment or action have any integrity—or any prospect of success.

Calvinism, of course, also subscribes to the doctrine of justification by faith (as it is often abbreviated, in part to stress the contrast to justification by works). But in a momentous decision as to the appropriate order of theological exposition, Calvin placed his discussion of regeneration or sanctification prior to his consideration of justification in Book III of his *Institutes of the Christian Religion*. Calvin is unambiguous in his insistence that God alone justifies the sinner—that justification is by divine grace, not by human works. Yet he is also concerned that utter reliance on the grace of God not be allowed to result in a passivity which countenances the continuance of evil in the lives of the faithful. Accordingly, he elaborates in considerable detail the character of regeneration and the Christian life in chapters three through ten of Book III before proceeding to a discussion of justification beginning in the eleventh chapter. And consistent with this ordering of his discussion, Calvin also revises Luther's tendency to see the law as simply negative, as only functioning to convict and punish the sinner and hence as standing radically in opposition to the Gospel. Beyond such negative uses, Calvin also espouses a positive interpretation of the law as ordering the life of the believer and of the Christian community so that it moves toward the visible realization of the rule of God and, in so doing, contributes to the divine glory.

A full exploration of the issues involved in this contrast between Lutheran and Calvinist orientations requires a movement beyond the polarities between existentialism and Zen. That further exploration will also entail criticism of the Lutheran position in particular. But with reference to the specific question of the respective emphases of the two traditions on justification and sanctification in the lives of believers, the parallels to the Zen and the existentialist perspectives are striking indeed. As with Zen, the Lutheran emphasis is on the assurance that the ultimate ontological context of the self is unconditionally accepting and, therefore, may be trusted or relied on absolutely. In contrast, the Calvinist shares with the existentialist a stress on the need for imagination and discipline as the self struggles so to fashion its existence that whatever of value is possible is in fact realized.

It is evident that there are genuine, indeed indispensable, strengths in both the Lutheran and the Calvinist positions—strengths which provide appropriate and at times necessary mutual correctives. Without the Lutheran emphasis on basic trust in the unconditional grace of God as the source of all constructive human responses, Calvinist concern with ethical action all too readily degenerates into moralism. And apart from the Calvinist insistence on the need for affirmative commitment to realizing the rule of God and thereby contributing to the divine glory, Lutheran concern with the issues of motivation and trust may result in indefensible passivity and quietism. Accordingly, the metaphor of rhythm between complementary strengths provides a more adequate image for approaching this complex of issues than does the attempt to assign absolute priority to one or the other.

As in the case of the polarities between existentialism and Zen, this metaphor of rhythm may then serve to underscore the fact that priority is a function at least in part of context. With respect to the most fundamental religious issue, the Lutheran emphasis is, I think, the right one. From the perspective of systematic reflection on the dynamics of the religious life, the question of ethical response presupposes an affirmative answer to the questions of trust in God and acceptance of the self. But in such contexts as collaborative work toward a definite ideal or goal, the Calvinist orientation rightly focuses on common action rather than concerning itself in the first instance with questions of motivation and trust. This focus is no doubt largely an expression of the urgency of the task at hand. But it also constitutes an at least tacit recognition that the relationship between faith as trust and faith as loyalty or commitment is a thoroughly dialectical one. Trust can and does generate commitment. But loyalty to a common cause can also lead to a growing faith in the sense of basic trust. As I have tried to argue in elaborating the truths of existentialism and Zen, Jesus' ministry as it is portrayed in the Gospel accounts moves between the same polar strengths: he seeks out the rejected of his time and proclaims the good news of God's grace and forgiveness, and he also announces the stringent demands of that rule of God which may be realized as the new life empowered through precisely this divine forgiveness and grace. In different contexts, one or the other emphasis is more prominent. But the two themes in any case mutually imply each other. To be adequate to the richness of the tradition, interpretations of Christian faith must, then, aspire to do justice to both emphases. The truth of Christianity is, in short, not less than the truths to which existentialism and Zen testify.

Christian Theology Beyond Existentialism and Zen

In the foregoing discussion of justification and sanctification as significantly parallel to the polarity between existentialism and Zen, I deliberately abstracted from the more inclusive soteriological dualities which Christian theology characteristically presupposes in addressing such issues. I am thinking here of such dualities as Fall/redemption, sin/salvation, and even old self/new self. Each of these dualities entails a movement from negative to positive. Hence the analogue in the terms of the preceding discussion would be movement from moral weakness or vice to strength or virtue. But I focused instead on polarities between strengths or virtues alone. The distinctions were accordingly all within the realm of redemption or salvation or the new self. The metaphor of rhythm is appropriate in that context; it calls attention to the need for complementary strengths. It would not, however, be apt in the more inclusive context, since it would in that case affirm and celebrate a movement back and forth between the negative and the positive.

This more inclusive context of movement from the old self or sin or the Fall to the new self or salvation or redemption is especially crucial for interpretations of Christian faith that express the third type. Indeed, systematic attention to precisely this movement construed as development over time is what distinguishes the alternative to existentialism and Zen. Accordingly, this question of programmatic concern with historical development serves to focus differences not only between certain Christian and some non-Christian perspectives, but also among contrasting positions within Christianity. Put cryptically and polemically, on this axis of comparison both existentialism and Zen have much in common with Lutheranism in contrast to an interpretation of Christian symbolism which expresses the third type and is more Calvinist.

To be less cryptic (though still polemical), what Lutheranism shares with existentialism and Zen over against the third type and Calvinism is a systematic disinterest in mediation. For existentialism and Zen, as those positions are generalized in this study, abstraction from temporal process is central to the very definition of the types. But Lutheranism displays a similarly pervasive aversion to construing historical development as centrally significant. For Luther and for Lutheranism the fundamental religious issue is radically atemporal: it is the question of the individual believer's immediate relationship to God, the question of whether or not one lives out of the trust that through divine grace one is justified. So emphatically central is this issue that other questions—those concerning ethics and the social order, for example—even though acknowledged as significant, are decidedly secondary. Accordingly, those issues can be safely assigned to the goverance of the princes, as they in fact are in the Lutheran conception of two kingdoms, one the province of the church and the other the responsibility of the secular order or the state.

In the case of similarities between Lutheranism and existentialism, the commonality is not simply a matter of systematic parallels. Rather, there are definite historical influences as well. Indeed, recent existentialism can be understood (I think appropriately) as a thoroughly secular version of Lutheranism. With the collapse of the ontologically transcendent reference of "historic religion," Lutheran insistence on the faithful life as grounded in the individual's right relationship to God is transposed into the existentialist concept of personal authenticity in the face of a neutral cosmos and an open future. But the underlying dynamics remain the same—especially with reference to the issue of how the individual is related to social and cultural development. To elaborate in detail the commonalities I am only adumbrating goes beyond the scope of this study. But the continuities in any case are patent in Kierkegaard's influence on virtually all twentieth-century existentialists, in Heidegger's direct relevance to Bultmann's theology, and, still more fundamentally, in the fact that all these thinkers share descent from Luther and Kant.

As a form of summary of the line of argument I have been advancing, it may be helpful to review the complex set of relationships that I contend obtain among existentialism, Zen, Lutheranism, Calvinism, and a Christian theology of the third type. The relationships are complex in part because two different axes of comparison are involved. The first distinction is, to use Christian language, between a position which emphasizes justification or faith as trust and one which stresses sanctification or faith as commitment. On this axis, there are, I argued in the preceding section of this chapter, significant parallels between Lutheranism and Zen on the one hand and Calvinism and existentialism on the other. And Christian theology expressing the third type of worldview must seek to affirm both emphases. There is, however, also a second axis of comparison: the extent to which a position interprets historical development as ultimately significant. In the language of Christian theology, the question in this case is whether or not development over time from the old self to the new self, from sin to salvation, from the Fall to redemption—indeed, finally, from creation to the eschaton—is a crucial focus for reflection. With regard to this axis of comparison, a Christian theology of the third type and Calvinism agree in an affirmative response. As I argued in some detail in elaborating the three types in the second and third chapters, this affirmation in turn entails a double relationship to existentialism and Zen: agreement with existentialism over against Zen that this change or development is a genuine moral transformation and not simply the product of a new point of view, and agreement with Zen over against existentialism that this change or development in the end refers to the whole of reality and not exclusively to dimensions of the individual's existence. Finally, in the case of Lutheranism, an individualistic focus that abstracts from more inclusive historical contexts is a definite tendency; and the doctrine of justification by faith alone at least lends itself to the interpretation that the crucial religious change is a new way of viewing one's relationship to God. Insofar as this double tendency is in evidence, Lutheranism thus exemplifies both of the disagreements and neither of the agreements that the third type has with existentialism and Zen.

   A Christian commitment that aspires to combine the strength of existentialism and Zen and to avoid the deficiencies exemplified in the Lutheran tendencies I have noted is, then, pressed to consider again the traditional affirmation of divine governance in and through the apparent anomalies and undeniable outrages of historical development, biological evolution, and cosmic process. The attraction of religious worldviews that avoid such affirmations is undeniable. In declining to make assertions for which it is clear what sorts of empirical data can count for and against, they do not run the risk of unnecessary and counterproductive quarrels with the natural and social sciences or, worse still, of contradicting the common sense of even those who would like to agree. Yet avoiding such affirmations entails a risk as well: that religious worldviews or commitments in the end become completely irrelevant to the world of everyday life in the sense that their acceptance or rejection makes no discernible difference. In any case, not only some (admittedly far from unambiguous) strains in the historical experience of humankind but also central commitments in the Christian symbol system as a whole testify to the potential for increased value in the natural and the historical order. So at least contend interpretations of the Christian tradition that illustrate the third type.

This affirmation of the potential for increased value in the natural and historical order does not entail a doctrine of inevitable progress. It does, however, require acknowledgment of the natural and historical order as the focus of religious concern and commitment. Expressed in Christian symbolism, this acknowledgment takes the form of affirming God and the rule of God as inextricably interrelated with the developing cosmos. Such ascription of central significance to natural and historical development need not and should not be construed as denying the increased and constantly increasing potential for destruction as well as for enrichment of life. But recognition of this double potential serves only to underscore the crucial significance of precisely the historical dynamics on which the third type focuses.

This affirmation of natural and historical development need not and of course should not entail a disparaging of attempts to interpret transformation in individuals. Put more positively, every adequate interpretation of Christian faith must attend to the dynamics of personal religious change. Only if that transformation is experienced and in turn reflected upon is there any interest in the more inclusive contexts of personal development. But to reflect on this personal change itself requires attention to those organizing images of faith and patterns of practice that transcend an exclusive focus either on the individual as such or on the individual in immediate relation to the cosmos or God. Otherwise theological reflection on personal transformation is cut off not only from much of the richness of the tradition but also from the dynamics of development in human history, in the biosphere, and even in the cosmos as a whole.

The Individual, Cult, and Community

The earliest records of the Christian church already testify to tensions that derive from a double commitment to individual freedom and to communal solidarity. Central to the good news as Paul expresses it in his letters is the fact of liberating transformation:

If anyone is in Christ, he is a new creation; the old has passed away, behold, the new has come. (II Cor. 5.17.)

Accordingly, the Christian is to "regard no one from a human point of view" and to resist being "conformed to this world" (II Cor. 5.16; Romans 12.2). As Paul himself puts it programmatically:

For freedom Christ has set us free; stand fast therefore, and do not submit again to a yoke of slavery. (Gal. 5.1.)

With respect to the specific issues that arose in the churches: believers should resist all attempts to require circumcision of Gentile converts; they need not honor one day more than another; nor do they have to abide by conventional canons of abstinence or purity in their eating— even to the point that there is in principle no objection to eating food offered to other gods. (Gal. 4 and 5, Romans 14, and I Corinthians 8 and 10 provide extended discussions of such issues.) But along with his radical proclamation of liberty, Paul also repeatedly invokes the norm of mutual upbuilding or the good of the neighbor:

"All things are lawful," but not all things are helpful. "All things are lawful," but not all things build up. Let no one seek his own good, but the good of his neighbor. (I Cor. 10.23-24. Compare I Cor. 8.7-13, Gal. 5.13-26, and Romans 14.13-27.)

There is, in short, radical freedom, but that freedom is in Christ—in one body that has many members, to use Paul's metaphor in I Corinthians 12.

In the history of Christian thought and practice, this double affirmation of the individual and the community has continued, though with striking variations in the relative priority accorded the two terms.[2] As the church became both more elaborately institutionalized and more pervasively Hellenized, the requirements of its corporate life received considerable attention. The Greek philosophical tradition provided resources for conceiving unities that encompassed pluralities within them so that, for example, the inclusion of all humankind in the human nature of Christ was intelligible. And Roman legal and organizational patterns contributed to the structuring of an imposing church order. Attention to the individual was certainly not absent. After all, it was the individual who was integrated into the community through its sacraments and polity. In Augustine, among others, there is, moreover, a systematic attending to personal experience as a theater of divine-human encounter. But such attention to the individual nonetheless occurred in the context of affirming the prior reality of the corporate body of Christ. Although the differences can easily be overstated, the mood of late medieval Nominalism, of the Renaissance, and of the Protestant Reformation stands in contrast to this position of the patristic and the early medieval church. While the community of saints was certainly still the assumed context in the piety and theology of this era, the Pauline theme of individual liberty received a renewed emphasis—an emphasis which subsequent Protestant development not only continued but at times increased to the point of allowing it to become a virtually exclusive preoccupation.

Already in Paul's exaltation of a liberty which calls into question every bondage to human convention the iconoclasm which this individualism entails is evident. It is an iconoclasm that has a long lineage before and after Paul: backward to the prophets of Israel, the covenant on Sinai, the Exodus, and the affirmation of the Genesis accounts that all of creation is good; and forward through the Reformation and Calvinism in particular, to those processes of secularization that have shaped modern western religious, economic, and political institutions. The connections in this lineage may seem more self-evident with respect to the parallels between Paul and the Jewish traditions which he presupposes than between all of the theological concerns including those of Calvinism and more recent secularizing trends. There are, of course, significant differences in the more recent developments; but the theme of iconoclasm nonetheless represents a crucial line of continuity.

Paul and the theological traditions he presupposes and in turn influences affirm that all of creation is good, that nothing is to be set aside as special or sacrosanct, that everything is therefore in principle allowed. Such use of the created order is to contribute to the glory of God, as Calvin puts it in re-emphasizing Paul's concern that the expression of individual liberty be ordered according to such criteria as those of mutual upbuilding and love of neighbor. But that glory is to be realized in all of life. Accordingly, worship of God may be expressed not only in the order that liturgy and polity articulate but also through personal service to one's neighbor and, for Calvin in particular, through disciplined activity in political and economic life. Hence the iconoclastic rejection of a separate or special religious sphere that follows from affirming God's governance in all of life is an impetus to what has come to be termed secularization. It is, in short, an iconoclasm that has contributed profoundly to both the power and the trauma of the West.

In the history of the West since the Enlightenment this individualizing and secularizing process has been expressed politically in democracy, economically in capitalism, and religiously first in Protestantism and then in a general toleration of diverse religious persuasions (including a special attraction for movements like existentialism and Zen which also are in some respects iconoclastic). In many Protestant churches the correlate of individualism and secularism has been a devaluation of the cultic and corporate dimensions of faith. In some instances this rejection of ritual has been programmatic, as in Puritan attacks on liturgical adornments as idolatrous. But even when ritual was not attacked directly, tendencies toward simplifying and rationalizing worship tacitly represented a similar dissatisfaction with whatever seemed to set religion apart as special or distinctive. Especially for such American denominations as Methodists, Baptists, Congregationalists, Presbyterians, and Unitarians, and for established Protestant churches like those in Germany, the result has not infrequently been services of worship that neither express the life of the community of faith nor nourish and support the individual believer.

Confronted with the pallid fare that may result from prophetic, Pauline, and Protestant iconoclasm, the attractions of a diet rich in ritual are powerful indeed. Those attractions no doubt account in part for the contemporary proliferation of highly stylized religious practice in varied and often exotic forms. A sampling of this tendency in the United States alone ranges from evangelical Protestant speaking in

tongues to Hare Krishna chant to Pentecostalist worship to Nichiren
Buddhist invocation to Roman Catholic requests for a return to the
Latin mass. Nor is there a dearth of sophisticated theoretical arguments for the value, indeed the indispensability, of ritual.[3] Yet despite the attractions, despite even persuasion of the enormous power
and potential value of ritual, there is no simple or direct access from
conviction as to the value of iconoclasm to a celebration of cult and
community.

The issue here may be concisely formulated with reference to Jewish and Christian symbolism about the Fall. In the account of Genesis
2 and 3, the contrast between the situation of Adam and Eve before
and after the Fall parallels the difference between ritual taboo and
self-conscious morality. After putting Adam and Eve in the garden,
God issues a categorical command:

You may freely eat of every tree of the garden; but of the tree of the
knowledge of good and evil you shall not eat, for in the day that you eat
of it you shall die. (Gen. 2.16-17.)

The serpent counters:

You will not die. For God knows that when you eat of it your eyes will
be opened, and you will be like God, knowing good and evil. (Gen. 3.4-5.)

Then the narrator reports that "the eyes of both were opened" (Gen.
3.7). From unreasoned ritual prohibition or taboo the account moves
to the emergence of human moral discrimination. There is in Christian theology a recurrent tendency to affirm this emergence into self-
consciousness—to interpret it as not only necessary but even salutary,
as a *felix culpa,* a fortunate Fall. Against visions of redemption as a
re-establishment of original righteousness, of the paradise before the
Fall, this tendency insists that the final consummation will exceed
that paradise in glory. At stake here is more than an abstruse issue
among obscure theologians; also involved is the fundamental psychological and cultural question of the extent to which the movement
from ritual to morality that the Genesis myth depicts is reversible.

The answer to this question is simply negative if reversing the
process means that iconoclastic adherents to the canons of a morality
that aspires to be autonomous must come to display an uncritical and
unreflective immersion in heteronomously imposed ritual. This highly

qualified response is, however, more an illustration of the problem than an indication of a solution. Precisely because a Protestantism and a secularism that value the ideal of autonomy have perceived all ritual as heteronomous, even as superstitious or magical, they have increasingly divorced themselves from the cultic and communal roots of faith. But participation in ritual need not be an exercise in heteronomy. Ritual does require disciplined action according to established norms. In this requirement, it is like language and other forms of communication. Submission to fixed patterns does not, however, in itself constitute heteronomy. Indeed, as is amply illustrated in the language arts or in music or in the visual and performing arts, only such submission in turn allows the creativity and freedom that the ideal of autonomy celebrates. Accordingly, it is possible that the movement from taboo to morality can be reversed in the limited sense that reflective and even self-critical human beings can also participate meaningfully in ritual patterns that they recognize as the product of cultural traditions for which they take responsibility.

Whether or not this reversal—or perhaps better, this further development—is realized in practice is in my judgment the single most momentous question facing religious communities in the West and increasingly also all over the world. It is, to be blunt, the question of the survival of such communities. As persons become more aware of the fact that all symbol systems are the expressions of human culture, are they still able to affirm their traditions even while they are prepared to criticize them? This question may, of course, be construed in very general terms. Then it asks about continuing interest in and even qualified assent to the interpretations of experience which religious systems provide. Since it seems highly probable at least for the forseeable future both that religious concerns or a religious dimension to life will remain and that such concerns will be articulated in some measure of continuity with past religious traditions, this query may, I think, safely be answered affirmatively. There is, however, also the more particular thrust of the question that asks about continued participation in differentiated religious communities. And the answer to this query is dependent not only on the preservation of recognizably religious ideas but also on the cultivation and enactment of distinctively religious practices or forms of life.

In the specific case of the Christian tradition, there are innumerable works—including this book—which argue for the truth of its symbol system. I for one am convinced that it is crucial for individuals to be delivered from their own self-centered preoccupations and to become committed to a community that is ultimately trustworthy and finally all-inclusive. I am also aware of this conviction as my own appropriation of Christian symbolism. But this abstract formulation has little power apart from the concrete communities that actualize its truth. As Christianity has always affirmed, this truth is preeminently attained in the love and service that is expressed in the lives of the faithful. It is, however, also both represented and realized in the ritual life of the community.

The two rituals that are most central to the Christian tradition are, of course, the sacraments of baptism and the eucharist. In both instances, there is a dramatic enactment of the individual believer's integration into an encompassing community that both supports and elicits commitment. In baptism, as it is interpreted in those communities that continue the ancient church's practice of celebrating this sacrament as an initiation rite for adults, and in the eucharist, or Lord's Supper, this dramatic enactment achieves special power because it involves the identification of the faithful with the dying and rising of Christ. In baptism believers thus appropriate their new identity through physically washing away the old self and allowing the new self to be born as they symbolically die and rise with Christ. And in the eucharist, celebration of the sacrament moves from confession through an identification with the brokenness and suffering of Christ represented or embodied in the bread and wine to a response of gratitude for the new life granted to the community of faith. In both rites there is, then, a movement from the bondage of isolation and self-centeredness to liberating participation in the community of those who seek to incorporate in their common life the power of the love expressed in and through Jesus' life and death—a love that conveys unqualified and ultimate affirmation through willingness to endure even the most extreme suffering so as to attract every individual to the rule or kingdom of God.

There are of course also other rituals in the Christian life. Prayer is a paradigm of disciplined attention that figures in virtually all Christian cultic activity. Hymn singing, chanting, testimonies, passing the peace, and many other more or less formalized activities are also significant rituals. In vital communities new ritual forms also develop as both the common life and the cause to which there is a collective commitment are celebrated. Such vitality cannot, however, be pursued as an end in itself. Nor is there much promise in deliberate attempts to invent ritual. There are, in short, no magic solutions in the sense of introducing completely novel rituals into communities that are erroneously claimed to be utterly bereft of them.

But what can be done is to counter such caricatures of cultic life as the suggestion that it requires heteronomous credulity, so that an authentic participation in ritual again becomes possible for those who have been in large measure divorced from its power. In this direction at least lies a hope that the impoverished liturgical life of many Protestant churches may become enriched through a renewed appreciation for the emphasis on sacramental mediation and corporate life evident in the ancient church and in Roman Catholicism through the centuries. So corrected, Protestantism may yet be able to play a role in resisting the corrosive individualism that ever more effectively isolates and also, paradoxically, standardizes contemporary men and women. It may, moreover, claim to re-establish the balance in the Pauline churches between Christian liberty and mutual upbuilding. In any case, this hope is superior to the alternative of settling for simply perpetuating the present pattern of malnutrition resulting from a diet that consists almost exclusively of words spiced only with a little music and, possibly, a friendly greeting.

Christianity and World Community

The orientation which Christian rituals express indicates the aim or intention of the religious life inasmuch as it is directed to the glory of God. However, as no one familiar with New Testament denunciations of parading religiosity before others needs to be reminded, the danger of ritual is that it comes to focus on itself or on the opinions of human observers rather than on that end to which it is ultimately directed. In a word, it becomes idolatrous—and therefore invites and requires iconoclasm.

One form in which the threat of idolatry is present in contemporary concern with ritual is precisely in the recognition of its power to shape and sustain a sense of community. This threat is a particularly complex and subtle one for traditions which include a tendency to construe ultimate reality to be social, as Christianity does. The doc-

trine of the Trinity as it is articulated and elaborated in the history of
theology testifies to this commitment in even the most traditional dogmatics. But the relevance of social symbolizations of the ultimate for
the question of human community is even more direct in those interpretations which self-consciously reject the traditional theological
conception of God as perfect and complete apart from the world.
In this case affirmation of the ultimate as social means that the attainment of value in history is construed as religiously central—as contributing to the fullness of the divine life. Accordingly, the temptation
to focus on developing a sense of community is very powerful. To
succumb to this temptation is, however, problematical on even the
most pragmatic premises, since community does not result from attempts to attain it as an end in itself. And on the premises of the
theological tradition, to focus exclusively on developing a sense of
community is not only an idolatrous denial of love for God but also
a reprehensible betrayal of love for neighbor inasmuch as it tends to
confine concern to one or another provincial affinity group.

Involved here are two issues, both of them central to a consideration of religious commitment in a pluralistic world. The first is how
Christianity, as one human tradition among others, may contribute to
the realization of world community in the sense of a just global order
committed to excluding no one from full participation. And the second is how even the most inclusive of human communities is related
to the divine reality Jesus points to in his parables about the kingdom
or rule of God. Even if a provincialism that uncritically exalts either
the Christian community or a particular culture is avoided, the issue
of idolatry remains with respect to humankind as a whole. Conversely, some approaches to countering the temptation to focus idola-
trously on the human may fail to support the development of historical communities that express what Paul terms mutual upbuilding and
love for neighbor.

Religious traditions at least appear to include impressive resources
for calling into question the tendency of every community to exalt existing prerogatives and perpetuate established interests. Perhaps the
most common indication of such resources is the role of religious
symbolization in mediating from the old to the new in critical periods
of transition for individuals and communities. In rites marking the
passage from youth to adulthood, for example, there is a process of
displacing one identity with another, a process that requires the call-

ing into question of established patterns and almost unavoidably entails awareness of dynamics common to the human as such. Awareness of the universally human is, of course, still more pronounced in the most inescapable of transitions: death. In the rites marking such fundamental thresholds, human symbolization frequently has recourse to imagery drawn from the life cycles of plants and animals, to representations of birds as connoting freedom, to the enduring qualities of earth and water. In short, the order of nature that underlies and transcends every culture may provide a certain critical distance over against established patterns. Indeed, the questioning of existing institutions may be even more direct, as in those rites that for carefully circumscribed periods break established social conventions—for example, eliminating or even reversing status distinctions, violating otherwise accepted sexual mores, or ridiculing ordinary role expectations.[4]

Yet despite this potential for a critical stance toward the established order, religious traditions all too frequently, even characteristically, serve more or less directly to legitimate the existing institutions of their respective historical contexts. Of the myriad considerations that bear on this failure to realize the potential for standing over against established interests, I want to call attention to two.

The first is no doubt self-evident, but nonetheless very important. It is that even in focusing on universal patterns, rites of passage perform a definite role integral to the structure of their particular society. When that role is vital, it may include the task of more or less self-conscious innovation as representative individuals or even all people for specified periods are allowed to disengage from routine activities for unencumbered reflection, meditation, and prayer, which then in turn may modify and in time profoundly influence existing social patterns. That role is, then, not to be denigrated. It is, however, still integral to the needs of a particular social order. When individuals move from youth to adulthood, for example, they do assume new identities. But no matter how radically rites celebrating this initiation into adulthood emphasize discontinuities both between the old and the new self-definition and between the ritual context and ordinary life, the intention of the participants is that individuals in the end accept the socially sanctioned identities to which they are introduced. Similarly, the fact of death may profoundly call into question various forms of provincialism. The role of rites of passage in this context is, however, not only to acknowledge realities that transcend each particular culture but also to re-integrate the memory of the deceased and the lives of the bereaved into the ongoing social process. Integration into established social structures is, then, one consideration that may help to account for the often very limited effectiveness of religious traditions in countering deficiencies in existing values and patterns of action.

The second consideration I want to mention is a closely related one, though it has to do more directly with variations in religious imagery and institutions. The spectrum of variation that I see as illuminating discriminates the different degrees to which religious symbolization provides resources for envisioning alternatives to established social structures. What is striking is that even the most trenchantly critical perspectives not infrequently offer relatively undeveloped resources for this constructive task. This limitation may, moreover, be expressed with reference to the typology elaborated in this study, inasmuch as existentialism and Zen illustrate positions in which visions of social life that might serve as alternatives to existing patterns play only a peripheral role. In contrast, recognition of the need for such visions is central to the third type.

I want to emphasize again that I am referring to existentialism and Zen as types. When the term is used to include such figures as Camus, there are certainly existentialists for whom social issues are prominent concerns. Similarly, in the case of Zen Buddhism, monastic life does provide a socially structured contrast to ordinary corporate life, even if its practice is dedicated to attaining an ahistorical perspective which is unconcerned about differences in social systems. With respect to this specific issue of envisioning social alternatives, the Zen type may accordingly be more clearly illustrated in those forms of Lutheran Christian or Vedāntic Hindu piety in which the individual's attainment of salvation or union with the ultimate is so central and so effectively integrated into the social order that the question of a transformation in society as a whole either does not arise at all or is addressed only as a separable and subordinate concern. But despite the need for historical qualifications, the systematic issue to which the types call attention is nonetheless significant. To conceive of the relationships between the aim of authentic or true life and common historical existence either as one of unqualified contrast (as existentialism does) or as one of undifferentiating inclusion (as Zen does) is, not surprisingly, less than fertile ground for germinating social visions.

Conversely, to interpret the attainment of a transformed corporate life as ultimately significant, as the third type does, places a premium on visions which may serve as standards for criticism and models for alternatives to established patterns.

Christianity shares with other religious traditions in the relative failure to stand over against the institutional patterns through which established interests exclude individuals and groups from unrestricted participation in the social order. Insofar as it has avoided both an uncritical legitimation of established social structures and an individualism which fails to envision corporate alternatives, its central resource has, however, been a conception of the church as a community provisionally differentiated from the secular order so as to signify and incipiently to realize the end for which creation as a whole is destined. In the Christian tradition, then, there have been strains both toward viewing the church as a kind of counterinstitution that resists complete subservience to the established social structure and toward envisioning a transformed corporate reality as the ultimate end to which the religious life is directed.

On the question of world community, such tendencies are not without their (at least rhetorical) disadvantages compared with existentialist and Zen motifs. For the advantage of both the existentialist and the Zen positions in regard to this question is precisely that their central concern with the individual and the ultimate allows the claim that they are relatively independent of particular historical communities and therefore may readily serve as the foundation for a universal world order. This claim is attractive in its apparent simplicity: through the straightforward proposal of focusing on the individual or the individual in unmediated relation to ultimate reality, the enormously complex if not insurmountable obstacle of cultural diversity is overcome. The attractions of this proposal are, however, deceptive if the ideal of world community is to be more than an aesthetically appealing abstraction. The reason is again simple and straightforward: the obstacles to world community include not only cultural diversity but also serious political and economic issues of social organization and resource distribution. And those issues cannot be addressed through abstraction from the complexity of historical dynamics.

The agenda of such issues is long indeed. Two complex and finally interrelated developments may, however, serve to epitomize the challenges confronting religious commitment that is serious about world community. The first is the troubling prominence in the last two decades of transnational or multinational corporations. And the second is the apparent conflict between the competing demands for environmental restraint and social justice.

What is perhaps most striking about the increasing vitality of transnational corporations in the decades since World War II is that this development has dramatized the need to have frames of reference other than that of a system of nation-states. This achievement stands in remarkable contrast to the very limited success of political, educational, and religious institutions in making the same point. To be blunt, the world seems far closer to an integrated economic order than to genuine institutional coordination on political, educational, or religious matters. To make this observation is not to glorify transnational business or to gloss over the abuses for which it is responsible. Nor is it to assume altruistic motives on the part of the managers of firms active in international markets. On the contrary, political control at both the national and international levels is imperative if countries, especially third world countries, are to be protected against the unscrupulous and indefensible practices that are possible through corporate manipulation of transnational resources and their accounting systems.[5] This imperative should not, however, be allowed to obscure the opportunity that the emergence of transnational corporations represents. For with all of the risks and uncertainties involved, this development may yet contribute to increasingly effective social and cultural cooperation as a response to the need to exert common control over economic institutions that are simultaneously a threat to the powerless and a demonstration of global interdependence. Both national and international efforts toward such control with particular reference to safeguards against exploitation of third world countries should accordingly be vigorously supported.

The emergence of at least apparent conflict between the claims of ecological crisis and social justice similarly illustrates the impossibility of engaging the question of world community without attending to the dynamics of historical development. There is no disputing the fact that the two claims conflict insofar as a central premise of much social welfare legislation is accepted. This premise is that continuing growth affords the hope of more for everyone without taking anything, or at least without taking very much, from those who already have enough. The increasing recognition that the earth's resources cannot sustain indefinitely continued economic growth means that on this premise the demands for social justice and environmental restraint are incompatible. The response need not, however, be confined to a choice of one or the other imperative. Rather, the premise must be rejected. Instead of placing hope for social welfare in proportionately the same slices of a larger economic pie, the recognition that it cannot grow indefinitely focuses the only alternative: to reslice the existing pie more equitably. Accordingly, those seriously committed to world community can no longer resist the conclusion that radical proposals for correcting the disproportion in existing patterns of resource allocation and use are the only defensible programs. The complexities which any such redistribution involves are staggering. It is also highly doubtful that there will be significant movement in this direction until further food, energy, and monetary crises force the issue. But because those further crises are sure to come, it is crucial that awareness of the need for redistribution counter indefensible and, in the end, counterproductive calls either for indifference or for retaliation.[6]

I am under no illusions that cryptic policy prescriptions of this sort can stand by themselves without further argument and detailed presentations of the relevant supporting data. My purpose in this context is, however, only to indicate the kind of concrete historical issues that unavoidably require attention if concern for world community is to be more than abstract. It is, in short, only to indicate representative and, I think, central items on the agenda for any serious pursuit of a socially just global order.

This formulation serves to focus the crucial question of who is to pursue this goal of world community. If the quest is to have any prospect of success, it will in the end have to enlist the cooperative efforts of political, educational, religious, and, yes, economic communities around the globe. But with specific reference to the Christian tradition, there is no excuse for anything less than immediate and energetic involvement. The demand for world community in the sense of a just global order committed to excluding no one from full participation is integral at least to those interpretations of the Christian tradition that affirm transformed historical life as of central religious significance. That transformation be on a global scale which excludes no one from full participation is for such interpretations continuous with the insistence of first-century churches that the community of faith exclude neither Jew nor Greek, neither slave nor free, neither male nor female. The parallel should not be allowed to obscure the dramatic differences that derive from being on opposite ends of the intervening nineteen centuries. But in both cases the community that is celebrated is in principle an open one and in aspiration all-inclusive.

Both this parallelism and the differences to which it calls attention suggest that the search for world community not only defines an urgent task for the church but also may help to clarify its own identity. Whatever vitality the church has in criticizing the self-serving actions of established interests continues to derive from its role as a community provisionally differentiated from the secular order so as to signify and, incipiently, to realize the destiny of all humankind. But increasing self-consciousness about the global context of the church in effect refocuses awareness of the character of the contrast to the secular order that is appropriate.

In the past this contrast has not infrequently been construed in effect in sociological terms: the church is less than the secular order in the sense that it is one differentiated sector—namely that concerned with religion—within a broader society. As a description of the social system, this representation no doubt has validity. But the church must also and with increasing clarity see itself as greater than, as more inclusive than, the states in which it is located. In this sense, the church stands over against the secular order as the harbinger of a world community which is in the process of emerging. Accordingly, the church can and should aspire to address the state from the standpoint of universal humankind rather than as one sub-set within a particular social system. In practice, this standpoint can and should express the needs of those whose voices are all to frequently not heard—as, for example, the World Council of Churches has in the last years increasingly tended to do. In time there can and should be genuine interaction and cooperation with other religious traditions that also seek to represent this standpoint. But so to act and so to speak is in any case an imperative of Christian symbolism—at least as it is interpreted in a theology expressing the third type.

God and the Kingdom of God

If the Christian tradition employs the resources that it has for countering inequities in existing patterns of international interaction, it may, then, contribute further to an emerging world community. But there remains the issue of idolatry with respect to humankind as a whole. After all, how does a celebration of world community differ from Feuerbach's insistence (in *The Essence of Christianity*) that the attributes predicated of God are in reality predicates of the human race?

A systematic response to this question requires a reiteration of the resources for affirming transcendence which positions of the third type share. That type does not posit a God who is a being, an absolute, perfect, and complete other who stands over against the world. In this sense there is agreement with Feuerbach that a literalizing of traditional symbolism about God is not defensible. The third type does, however, affirm transcendence in insisting that no finite person or object or community is ultimate but is rather integral to an encompassing reality that alone is worthy of final trust and loyalty. The finite is, in short, relativized through the true infinite: that reality which excludes nothing from its life and accordingly can be conceived only dynamically, only through a process which is intrinsically self-critical in the sense that it forever calls itself into question precisely because otherwise it would be delimiting, the concept of only another finite entity. Even universal human community is, then, an idol insofar as it is absolutized. For the human community is still one finite reality among others and hence must be emphatically distinguished from the true infinite.

In its use of the concept of the true infinite, this formulation is, of course, Hegelian. I employ this concept because I think it is especially effective and impressively elegant in its argument against all forms of idolatry. I want, however, to reiterate my observation in the third chapter that Hegel's thought is only one example—though admittedly a very powerful one—of the alternative to existentialism and Zen in recent western philosophy and Christian theology. Some other instances stand directly under his influence: Marxism, for example, or a communitarian philosophy like that of Josiah Royce or Christian theologies like those of Wolfhart Pannenberg and Hans Küng. Independent of and prior to Hegel is the impressive theological work of Jonathan Edwards, who systematically appropriated Augustinian-Calvinist traditions so as to focus their commitment to the role of creation in contributing to the glory of the creator. More recent Christian theology cannot claim to be independent of Hegel's influence; frequently the connections are, however, only indirect, combined with other traditions that appear more prominently, and hence in any case often not centrally acknowledged. Both process theologies and theologies of liberation illustrate this pattern.

In the case of process theologies the systematic parallels to Hegel's position are striking indeed even when, as with Whitehead himself, the direct influences are minimal. With all their differences, an agenda common to philosophers like Whitehead and Charles Hartshorne and theologians like Daniel Day Williams, John Cobb, and Schubert Ogden is to criticize what they term classical theism and commend dipolar theism in its place. And the force of this criticism is precisely to reject every conception of God as complete and perfect apart from the world. The divine attributes as they are elaborated in the conceptuality of classical theism are not simply denied. God is eternal and unchangeable. This fact of abstract structure that includes all patterns of possible meanings and values does not, however, exhaust the divine reality. It is instead only the primordial nature of God. There is also the consequent nature of God: that reality which is fully related to the world and intrinsically involved in its movement toward increased value.

Theologies of liberation similarly illustrate an emphasis on the crucial import of transformation in the historical order. The resources on which liberation theologians draw reflect the diversity of their personal, social, and cultural contexts. For James Cone, those resources include a central concern with black religious traditions and a decisive influence from the thought of Karl Barth. For Gustavo Gutierrez, there are special debts both to Latin American political thought and practice and to Roman Catholic theological and exegetical traditions. For Dorothee Sölle, modern European literature, along with recent German theology and philosophy, figures prominently. But despite this diversity and the undeniable effects it has, there is a common focus on and through central Christian images for social liberation and cosmic fulfillment: Exodus, divine identification with suffering and oppression as it is expressed in the life and death of Jesus, eschatological consummation of the whole of creation. Typically in concert with Marxist conceptuality, this complex of themes becomes the medium for confessing the ultimate significance of historical transformation.

I am not proposing that all such philosophical and theological tendencies are simply interchangeable—or even that they all unambiguously illustrate the third type as I have outlined it. Insofar as process thought, for example, continues to use and defend traditional language about God as a personal being, it does not illustrate the third type (and also is not, in my judgment, internally coherent). Similarly, insofar as the Barthian substratum evident in Cone's early works persists even in *God of the Oppressed,* he does not illustrate the third type (and likewise in my reading has problems of coherence). All these strains in recent philosophy and theology do, however, illustrate the depth and breadth of concern in recent western and Christian thought with the issues on which the third type systematically focuses.

The third type in both its Hegelian and related forms is, then, not without resources for affirming transcendence historically conceived. To indicate such resources is, however, only a general response to the question of comparison to Feuerbach's celebration of the divinity of the human race. As has frequently been illustrated throughout the foregoing exposition, in my own more particular appropriation of Christian symbolism the governing image for interpreting this transcendence is that of the kingdom or rule of God. I interpret this image as referring to the encompassing context that supports and shapes the faithful individual, committed communities, and finally the cosmos as a whole. My approach illustrates the third type in that I do not speak of God as a being or an entity conceived as separate from the world. Instead, the reality of the divine rule in the end includes all that is. To use the language of the tradition to register a contention that it does not make, there is no God apart from the kingdom of God. I believe that this contention can do justice to the central thrust of Jesus' parables about the kingdom. But I do not advance it on this authority alone. Instead, it seems to me to follow from a central fact about increasing ranges of contemporary life and thought: that propositions about a transcendent personal being who intervenes on request in nature and history are not compelling even to many who nominally subscribe to them.

The lack of resonance between such propositions and the experience of many persons today is, of course, an illustration of the collapse of the dualism presupposed in what Bellah terms "historic religion." Acknowledgment of this collapse can be and frequently is resisted under the banner of opposing acquiescence to the conventional wisdom of current cultural trends. The problem with marshaling resistance on this front is, however, that it entails typically reactionary alliances on strictly theoretical issues that nonetheless may entail undesirable practical consequences. Whether or not God is a personal being who intervenes in nature and history in response to individual supplications cannot be adjudicated, though this belief may result in an unfortunate quietism. Whether or not there is personal subjective immortality likewise does not allow adjudication; but assent to this proposition may lead to a definite disengagement from historical life and a regrettable self-exaltation of the individual.

Affirmation of such propositions may no doubt also support an attractive assurance grounded in a confident trust in God and an effective resistance to deifying existing human communities. These virtues may, however, be just as powerfully exemplified in commitments that illustrate the third type. In this systematic alternative the ultimate ontological context of human life is also affirmed as trustworthy, and human individuals along with the finite communities in which they participate are construed as integral to and finally also subordinate to an encompassing process that elicits their loyalty and faithfulness. But in contrast to the tendency evident in the interpretations that continue to illustrate "historic religion," this complex of strengths also radically supports and nourishes engagement in the process of historical transformation.

Like other approaches to Christian symbolism, this alternative still confronts the most intractible of all facts in human experience: the reality of suffering and evil. Especially in the face of the enormity of willful destructiveness that Auschwitz and Hiroshima represent, there can never be any easy answers here. Indeed, as the Book of Job has testified over the centuries, there is no theoretical solution to the problem of evil that is anything but offensive to humane sensibilities. In practice, all that is either possible or appropriate is to resist evil. And this resistance in both active and passive forms is central to the Christian symbolism on which the third type focuses. In the figure of Jesus as embodying the rule of God, it affirms the reality of divine grace and liberation and the demand which that reality entails: so to identify with the sick and the oppressed that they may be healed and set free through the power of the suffering love expressed in the life and death of Jesus and integral to the divine life itself. And in the eschatological image of the kingdom of God, it rejects every final acquiescence to evil as unworthy of that ultimate community in which every opposition to the divine rule is overcome.

A striking representation of this combined trust and commitment is the vision of the new Jerusalem with which the Christian scriptures close. The vision epitomizes the commitments systematized in the third type. Consequently, it may serve to provide not only a concluding summary but also a final acknowledgment of the dependence of typological abstractions and generalizations on the concrete imagery of particular traditions. In his vision, the writer of the Book of Revelation describes "a new heaven and a new earth":

And I saw the holy city, new Jerusalem, coming down out of heaven from God, prepared as a bride adorned for her husband; and I heard a great voice from the throne saying, "Behold, the dwelling of God is with men. He will dwell with them, and they shall be his people, and God himself will be with them; and he will wipe away every tear from their eyes, and death shall be no more, neither shall there be mourning nor crying nor pain any more, for the former things have passed away." (Rev. 21.2-4.)

In the final chapters of the Bible there is, then, a reaffirmation of the divine sovereignty over nature and history. In the end the rule of God, present as the power of creation and expressed in committed individuals and communities through the centuries, governs the new order which it establishes. In this new order, the visionary of the Book of Revelation reports, there is no temple. For the divine rule is in that eschatological order at last omnipotent and omnipresent. There the Christian utopia is realized: God is all in all.

Notes

1. For a recent summary review of this complex of historical issues with specific reference to contemporary Jewish-Christian relations, see John T. Pawlikowski, "The Contemporary Jewish-Christian Theological Dialogue Agenda," *Journal of Ecumenical Studies,* XI (1974), pp. 599-616, esp. pp. 608-11. For more detailed interpretations of the historical data, see Louis Finkelstein, *The Pharisees* (Philadelphia: Jewish Publication Society, 1964), 2 vols.; and Jacob Neusner, *From Politics to Piety: The Emergence of Pharisaic Judaism* (Englewood Cliffs, N.J.: Prentice-Hall, 1973).
2. For a more detailed exposition of differences that I refer to only in passing here, see my *Christologies and Cultures: Toward a Typology of Religious Worldviews* (Atlantic Highlands, N.J.: Humanities Press, 1974), chaps. 3

and 4. The distinction I develop there between Realism and Nominalism is especially relevant.

3. For a concise and provocative summary statement, see Evan M. Zuesse, "Meditation on Ritual," *Journal of the American Academy of Religion,* XLIII (1975), pp. 517-30. A more sustained, even unrelenting, critique of what she terms "anti-ritualism" is Mary Douglas, *Natural Symbols* (New York: Random House–Vintage Books, 1973). Intriguing as her argument is, it seems to me seriously deficient precisely in its systematic failure to take account of the extent of which the processes of secularization at least appear to be irreversible.

4. In the vast literature on this complex of questions, a recent collection of essays that is especially provocative is Victor Turner, *Dramas, Fields, and Metaphors: Symbolic Action in Human Society* (Ithaca: Cornell University Press, 1974), esp. pp. 23-59, 166-299. The four essays to which the pages indicated refer include theoretical reflections that are a definite advance over Turner's less qualified views in *The Ritual Process: Structure and Anti-Structure* (Chicago: Aldine Press, 1969).

5. To note the obvious, I am in this very cryptic formulation summarizing a position that would require volumes of data and argument to defend even inadequately. Two helpfully complementary volumes that provide an overview of the issues are Richard J. Barnett and Ronald E. Müller, *Global Reach: The Power of Multinational Corporations* (New York: Simon & Schuster, 1974), and Raymond Vernon, *Sovereignity at Bay: The Multinational Spread of U.S. Enterprises* (New York: Basic Books, 1971). As different as are the tone and the ranges of data on which they draw, the two books provide surprisingly similar sets of recommendations.

6. Mihajlo Mesarovic and Eduard Pestel, *Mankind at the Turning Point: The Second Report to the Club of Rome* (New York: E. P. Dutton and Reader's Digest Press, 1974), is an attempt to represent the complex interactions that must inform any policies with respect to global development in the context of ecological constraints. In its attention to regional differences and to the issue of reducing the economic gap between rich and poor regions, this study is a definite advance over its predecessor, Dennis L. Meadows *et al., Limits to Growth: A Report for the Club of Rome's Project on the Predicament of Mankind* (New York: Universal Books, 1972).

Index

111